FLY FISHING
— *the* —
SOUTHEAST
COAST

FLY FISHING
— *the* —
SOUTHEAST
COAST

A Complete Guide to Fishing Fresh and Salt Water

GORDON CHURCHILL
FOREWORD BY RIP WOODIN

Skyhorse Publishing

Skyhorse Publishing books may be purchased in bulk at special discounts for sales promotion, corporate gifts, fund-raising, or educational purposes. Special editions can also be created to specifications. For details, contact the Special Sales Department, Skyhorse Publishing, 307 West 36th Street, 11th Floor, New York, NY 10018 or info@skyhorsepublishing.com.

Skyhorse® and Skyhorse Publishing® are registered trademarks of Skyhorse Publishing, Inc.®, a Delaware corporation.

Visit our website at www.skyhorsepublishing.com.

10 9 8 7 6 5 4 3 2

Library of Congress Cataloging-in-Publication Data is available on file.

Cover design by Tom Lau
Cover photo courtesy of the author

ISBN: 978-1-5107-1499-1
Ebook ISBN: 978-1-5107-1501-1

Printed in China

Dedicated to my family—they've been putting up with this for years.

Contents

Acknowledgments

According to the Rolling Stones, "We all need someone we can lean on." My wife, Melissa, is the best. She has supported me through this whole process. Without her I would not have been able to write this book. She has been patient when I've been out "researching" and "collecting data," and she's always been enthusiastic about helping with experiments in the kitchen afterward. They don't make many people better than Melissa.

I hope your father went all out for you like mine did for me.

My father, Don Churchill, always had time to take me fishing. Whether it was to fool walleye on Oneida Lake in New York, or to accompany me on a fly-fishing trip anywhere, he was there. It's been my pleasure to share my experience with my dad by hooking him into a big false albacore, speckled trout, or redfish. There is also the rest of my family who have put up with my fishing-obsessed mind for so long—BJ Churchill, Judi Harper, Rick Harper, Katie Lee, and Eamon Lee. My kids, Ella and Will, who know more about fishing than most kids ever dreamed of at their age, if only through osmosis and listening to phone conversations.

There are many folks who helped me along the way—some who aren't around anymore. Most notable was Pete Allred. He befriended me, sharing knowledge from his stool behind the counter at Pete's

The author and his daughter, Ella, enjoy their time on the water together.

Tackle in Morehead City, North Carolina. There was a fun gang of addicted anglers who spent a lot of time there, and some of them are gone now too. I think of them often.

Some other great guides and anglers have been there through the years as well. The sharing of information among anglers is really what helps the sport grow, and makes individual anglers better. Some I still talk to almost every day, and some I don't. Guys like Tom Roller, Richard Stuhr, Bill Douglass, Pete Paschall, Scott Sherron, Rip Woodin, Bryan Pahmeier, Lee Dunn, Chris Ellis, Ryan Rice, Jack Brown, Neill Pollock, Daniel Griffee, Dave Bernstein, Derek Brock, Tyler Cluverius, John Nguyen, Sean Fitzpatrick, David Edens, and Richard Ehrenkaufer make us all better.

We'll discount the fact that Rip Woodin is a Carolina fan because he can fish.

I can't forget some people who have helped me with my writing over the years, like my high school English teacher, Dorothy Baker; others include Steve Peha, Margot Lester, and Monte Burke.

If you find folks who will share with you as much as you share with them, hold onto them, for that is a rarity. If you have family who share your passion, count that as a true blessing.

There's nothing better than getting two sweet kids together on a boat.

Foreword

I was a trout fisherman before I met Gordon Churchill. After moving back to the Tar Heel state from northern Michigan, and Wyoming before that, I traded my fly rod and size 18 flies for a tennis racket and golf clubs since there were no trout streams in eastern North Carolina.

After a decade without fishing, my wife wanted a duplex on Atlantic Beach, so part of the deal was I got a little boat and an 8-weight fly rod. I quickly learned that fresh- and saltwater fly fishing have nothing but the principle in common. The saltwater rods are heavier, the flies bigger, the fish much larger, the wind higher, and the casting harder.

I'd been out with several guides, caught a few fish, but hadn't learned much. Enter Gordo. I found his blog about stalking redfish in the spartina grass at high tide. Sight fishing sounded great, bringing back memories of fooling a 16-inch rainbow on the Henry's Fork in Idaho. I didn't do that very often, but the excitement of seeing a trout drift up under my fly was heart stopping. That was until Gordon put me on an 8-pound redfish, sunlight winking off its tail, wagging above the water line as it rooted for a crab on the bottom.

My education in Professor Churchill's class began. First, it was casting without hooking him on the poling platform. Then, tying a non-slip loop knot so his crabby/shrimpy fly would twitch enticingly. I had a problem with the "trout strike" that freshwater fly rodders usually bring to the salt. One time we were on a flat near Morehead City when we saw a huge red up against the shoreline, pushing grass aside as it cruised the buffet line. I put the fly in front of the fish, it ate, and I gave a mighty trout set. Pop. The 12-pound nylon broke like 7X trout tippet.

"Dude, you just lost the biggest red we've seen all year. That trout set looked like you were striking on a tuna!" Gordon doesn't mince words. After that, I whispered "strip strike, strip strike" every time I cast to a fish.

Gordon has proved a person doesn't have to grow up in coastal North Carolina to be a good guide. When he moved south, Gordon brought a technical base of knowledge from fishing upstate New York all his life. Learning from the old salts willing to help a brash but humorous Yankee, he started guiding for false albacore.

The rigors of being a full-time ocean guide and having a growing family forced him to think creatively. He researched how tailing redfish were pursued in South Carolina, which had an innovative guiding community. Gordon put a platform on a beat-up johnboat before he got his Ankona Copperhead microskiff and took clients on the myriad flats off the Intracoastal Waterway. Word got around.

Within a few years, Gordon had shared his skinny-water secrets with a few captains who began showing up on the flats in their own technical skiffs. Other guides weren't the only people to notice the new fishing grounds. Commercial fishermen, long at odds with rec-reational anglers, began setting nets at the mouths of creeks, harvest-ing schools of redfish as "by-catch" to flounder fishing. Instead of seeing eight or ten fish on a trip to the flats, the number dropped to five, then three.

One beautiful late afternoon, we found a nice-sized red floating dead in the water. Gordon hauled it out to show me the fresh diamond-shaped marks on the fish where it had been entrapped by a large mesh gill net. The netter probably caught more redfish than allowed and tossed this smaller one to keep the larger fish. "It's so wasteful," he said, adding several expletives to describe how North Carolina poorly manages its fish resources. "We're the only state on the Atlantic and around to Texas that allows so much inshore gill netting," he explained.

So besides learning to fish a little better, Gordon Churchill got me interested in conservation. He was an early voice for responsible fisheries management. He was posting videos of wanton gill net destruction on YouTube shortly after the popular website opened. A few guides agreed with his fiery crusade, but most didn't want to earn the emnity of the commercial crowd. Now there is hope for meaningful reform since the political pendulum of fisheries management appears to be swinging away from the prior "harvest every fish" mentality.

Anglers can still take classes from Professor Churchill by following the tips in this book, which reflects his belief in sharing fishing knowledge, just as the old salts did with him years ago. We don't fish as guide/client any more. I grin at his vociferous opinions on everything from ACC basketball to politics, and am glad to count myself among his friends.

—Rip Woodin

Chapter One

The Scenario

The alarm goes off at zero dark thirty. Instead of punching the snooze, your feet hit the floor in seconds. It's not a workday. You're going fishing. As you brush your teeth, you start running through your preparations. Flies tied? Check. Rods rigged with new leaders and flies? Check, check. Boat gassed up? Definitely.

A sunrise like this portends great things to come.

Sandwiches and drinks? Yup. You get a text from your buddy: "On the road." You'll be meeting up with him in about 30 minutes. The boat trailer is already hooked up. Grab your coffee mug and out the door.

Pole to those fish.

Arriving at the ramp, your buddy is already there. He's juiced up on caffeine and breakfast sandwiches too. Launch the boat and blast off from the ramp. It's about a 40-minute cruise to the fishing grounds this morning. You sit back and enjoy the ride. The sunrise is gorgeous over a clear, azure sky. The wind is barely stirring. You instinctively know the way through the narrow channels and deeper parts of the flats. About a quarter-mile away, you shut down. Early morning fish don't put up with engine noise. It's too shallow to use a trolling motor so you pole. It's not too far and the effort will pay off.

A Splash and a Pop

When you're about 150 feet away, you see the first sign of life. A nice splash with a popping sound is a sure indicator of a feeding fish. Small minnows are schooling up against the shoreline. Your fishing buddy has a small streamer tied on that is a perfect match for these baitfish. About 80 feet out he starts his first cast. He drops it on the edge of the baitfish school and starts his retrieve. It's then that you look a little farther out and see the fish, several dozen in the 6- to 9-pound range. "Pick up and cast again. Eleven o'clock. Ninety feet. Point your rod tip."

The first run is intoxicating.

Just as he points, there is another smack. "I got it." He throws a really nice cast right in there. Strip, strip. Tight line. Strip strike. Fish on! First fish of the day. The first run takes it right away from the shoreline and into slightly deeper water. You smile and take pictures of your buddy working the fish. It finally comes to the boat after a spirited fight. He has a bit of a struggle getting his hand around it at boatside and gets splashed in the face. That makes for some chuckles. You get a couple hero shots. He mugs for a selfie to send his wife or post on Instagram. "Your turn now bro," he says.

You gladly relinquish the push pole. As you gracefully (maybe *not* gracefully) navigate around opposite sides of the microskiff to reach the bow, you can tell the fish are still there. But now you're up, and you've got a small popper on one of your rods. Your buddy softly speaks, "There they are, 12:00 o'clock." You get up on the very point of the bow and false cast—once, twice, and shoot your fly toward the feeding fish. Pop . . . Pop . . . Pop . . . Slurp. Strike. Fish on again. The fact that this is a bigger fish is immediately apparent since it's into your fly-line backing in a matter of seconds and is heading for the horizon. You take your time and let the fish do its thing. As long as you don't do anything like clamp down on the reel or the hook doesn't pull for some reason, you'll catch this fish. The hardest parts—knowing where to go, how to get there, how to approach, what fly to use, how to cast, and how to present the fly—are all done. Now you just enjoy having done it all correctly.

This Isn't Far-Fetched

Do you like this scenario? Does it seem far-fetched? It's not. Happens every day. You don't have to go to the Bahamas or some other exotic island to catch a big fish on a fly, you can do it right in North Carolina, South Carolina, or Georgia. A geographical range from the southern end of Pamlico Sound, North Carolina, in the north to St. Augustine, Florida, in the south is marked by warm southerly currents and marshes ringed with spartina grass. Much farther up the coast, the northerly currents predominate, and the striped bass holds

One of Chris Ellis's favorite things about fishing is going to the places they live.

sway inshore. Below St. Augustine, you get into mangrove creeks with snook and tarpon.

Our type of fishing is never easy. Neither is calculus, but it's important, and this is way more fun. You need to know what species you want to target, what rod and line combo works best, which flies to stock, and most important, where and when to do it. The only thing I'm not going to give you here is specific places to go. You should be able to put enough pieces together to find locales that will work for you. If you get all those right, then you can still mess it up if you can't present the fly properly. It's why we play the game. Otherwise what's the point, right? We could just chunk a hunk of meat out there. But no, we'll do this the right way. Learn all the variables, put them together, practice our casting, get out on the water, and catch a nice fish on a fly.

Just can't beat it.

We're going to start inshore and work our way all the way out to the Gulf Stream. (I'm assuming basic knowledge here of knots, leaders, and casting. If you need help with those, there are other books I will recommend.) I have fly fished the Atlantic Seaboard from Cape Cod to Key West, but the focus of this book is along the coasts of North Carolina, South Carolina, Georgia, and North Florida primarily. It is a land of spartina marsh that has not been taken over by exotic plant species like you'll often find further south. The climate is moderate due to southerly water currents, and you can fish twelve months a year. The fish species that you can target are pretty consistent along this whole stretch of the Southeast. The way to approach them is consistent everywhere and we will focus on that approach.

Chapter Two

Largemouth Bass

It was a perfect evening. The frogs were croaking, the crickets chirping. It was the third of July, and my regular fishing partner, Griffin, with whom I normally fish at this pond, was out of town with his parents. Oh yeah, he's the thirteen-year-old son of a best fishing buddy. We were here a week prior and spooked a really nice fish in a shallow corner of the pond. The only things around to see me now were some goats and an old horse. I stood back about 30 feet from the edge and stripped about 60 feet of line onto the grass and started to false cast. After I had all the line out, I dropped my little hand-crafted popper onto the surface in that corner. *Pop. Pop. Pop. Bloosh!* There he was! It was a really nice fish of about 3 pounds. It gave a little run out into the middle and jumped, earning a nine from the judges. It hung in the air for a second to give me a nice image to remember. I worked him in, snapped a quick photo with my smartphone, and laid him in the water. He hovered there for just a second then darted off. What a perfect start. It was even better when I sent the picture to my buddy and told him to show his son while they were stuck in the car.

That was a nice evening.

Golf Course Ponds

Near the coast, my favorite place to fish for largemouths is in golf course ponds. There is something perfect about watching the life around the pond on a gorgeous spring or summer evening as I toss a popper into the bassy spots. It's serene as the sun sets, but then the water explodes when a 5-pound bass comes out of nowhere to attack the popper. That's pretty cool. It's also a really great way to practice your casting and get a kid interested in fly fishing. There's not a lot of wind to deal with, you don't need a boat, and you can stop anytime you want to just hang out and goof off. That's usually what kids like to do anyway.

Put a fly rod in their hands.

The Equipment

Start with a 6-weight fly rod. You can use heavier if you want, but most of the fish you catch will be less than 5 pounds so there is no need for a bigger stick. When I have tried a lighter rod, it becomes a chore to cast the poppers and buggy flies I like to use. A floating fly line will do perfectly. For flies, I like to use a popper most of all. Make sure you bend the hook barb flat to facilitate an easier release. Pond bass really respond well to poppers beginning during spawning time in early spring right through summer. When they are on the beds thinking about love, they hate anything floating over them. In the summer, careless frogs swimming on the surface get eaten, so the popper that mimics them gets nailed. It's really what fly fishing is all about.

Homemade popper, homemade bamboo rod.

The Technique

Your first cast should be right against the bank where you are going to be fishing. Stop 10 yards from the shoreline, then drop your fly in the water right in front of where you are planning to stand. There is nothing worse than walking up to a pond and watching a nice fish swim away from you. Not until you have covered the area in front of you should you approach the bank.

Next cast down the shoreline, working around the pond like a clock. It's an old cliché that you should work the water along the shoreline first before casting out in the middle, but old fishing clichés get tossed around because they usually are true. A strike could happen at any time. Keep your rod tip low and strip your line sharply to make the fly pop. I don't like to make a huge splash. Remember the

Stand back from the water for your first cast or the first fish you see will be silently swimming away.

water is shallow; any kind of noise will be noticed. When a fish hits, strip-strike with your line hand, try not to lift too much with the rod until you feel the weight of the fish.

After you hook up, you'll get a nice jump or two. You should be able to play the fish by stripping it in with your hand. I don't like reeling in loose line unless it's a big bass that takes most of it out. They always seem to get off when I do that. When you get the fish to your feet, grasp its lower lip and lift it straight up without bending its lower jaw down like the bass pros do on television. This hurts the jaw. Pop the hook out, then watch it swim away: A perfect time.

"Dad, can we fish today?"

My daughter, Ella, was catching the fishing bug. "Dad, can we go fishing today?" There is only one appropriate answer to that question. She had been catching some small bass on a little spinnerbait with a push button rod. She really wanted to get one with a fly rod. I started her out in a spot where the sunfish were swarming around a drainage pipe. She had a natural casting inclination and was throwing 30-foot casts sooner than a lot of adults would. The little wet fly she was using was an easy mark for the sunnies. I had her slowly skate it across the surface so they'd hit it. This was how she caught her first fish ever on a fly. Next was the bass. I put on a small grasshopper fly. She cast it along the shoreline as we walked along. There were so many small bass in the pond that I knew it was just a matter

Proud kid.

of time. And it sure was. Her first bass on a fly was about 10 inches long. She grabbed its lower jaw, holding it up for a picture just like a pro. Awesome!

The most difficult part of pond bassing is finding a pond to fish. Check mapping apps to see what's there. Hit up friends and family who live on golf courses. Or even do what one friend of mine has done. He actually got a membership at a country club pool, ostensibly to go swimming, but mainly to fish the ponds on the back nine in the early morning. Always check with the pro shop. Explain that you'll move off when golfers get close. The answer may still be no, but it's better than being chased off by a red-faced guy in a golf cart.

Alternative Locations

There are other places and ways to bass fish on the coast. Largemouths live in cypress swamps and rivers, which can be great places to fish in the spring before the shad runs start. I don't do much of it anymore, but they can be targeted with big streamer flies. You'll need a weed guard of some kind because you'll be casting back under cypress knees. It can be great fishing. It's not uncommon to catch dozens in a day.

On the Roanoke River near Williamston, North Carolina, the boat ramp is next to the paper mill. It didn't smell very good that morning, but we weren't there for very long. We took off upriver at 60 miles per hour in my friend's sparkling bass boat. We came to a side creek and made a long, sweeping turn in. After another five minutes, we came off plane. Thirty minutes at 60 miles per hour gets pretty chilly in February. My friend is a bass-fishing maniac, complete with bait-casting reels and soft plastic jerk baits. I had a variety of big streamers with guards to protect them from getting caught in the cypress branches overhanging the water.

Using an 8-weight rod with floating line, I put my streamer—a really wiggly one called a Snake Fly—as tight to the branches as I could. The first strike was a shock. I was still pretty chilled but the fish warmed me up. It was a steady parade of 3- to 5-pound bass all day. I had one on that was considerably bigger but he got me into the bushes. It seems like a typically exaggerated fish story, but that's how it goes.

When you let a nine-year-old take photos, you get unique perspectives.

Even though you don't hear much about it because of nearby saltwater fisheries, largemouth bass fishing in coastal areas can be very good. I've heard good things about residential ponds and golf course ponds in South Carolina. Look out for alligators. Check your maps. Look around as you're driving. If you see a pond, a quarry, small lake, or freshwater river near the coast, it might be worth a check.

Chapter Three

Hickory Shad

An inflatable boat, canoe, or kayak is the way to get away from the crowds and catch some fish.

The Roanoke River is known regionally as a hotspot for shad fishing. People flock to Weldon, North Carolina, in droves every spring to get their shad groove beginning in late February and on through April. Standing at the Weldon boat ramp,

A shad makes his way upstream through some shallow water.

you can see dozens of people and just as many boats in that short stretch of river. You can even catch shad right at the ramp if you like combat fishing. If that isn't very appealing, there is another way. With a canoe or kayak, you can fish the river upstream of Weldon. You will catch just as many fish, if not more, and see hardly any people because the rocks stop power boats. You will also witness thousands of shad in the shallow riffles. They swim across the tops of the rocks with their backs and tails out of the water, which really lets you take a nice long look at them.

When the water is low, the easiest way to fish upstream of Weldon is to take a canoe and launch it underneath the US-301 highway bridge in Weldon. "The Rockfish Capital" bridge has a dirt path alongside it that runs right to the river. It's a simple matter to drive down and launch a canoe or other cartop boat. There is a big, deep pool above the Weldon rocks where shad will stack up. Use a sinktip or sinking fly line to reach them. You can also paddle upstream quite a ways since the water is quite flat. Fish will often be found from above The Rocks all the way up to the first big drop off upstream. If they are there, they'll be rolling.

Another Low-Water Option

The hat is what really makes this picture.

If you really want to get away from people, there is another option. What I used to do when the water was really low, below 8,000 cubic feet per second on the river gauges, was launch a raft at the wildlife ramp in Gaston, off State Highway NC-48. At this ramp you can float almost the entire rocky part of river from where it comes out of the Roanoke Rapids Dam canal, then down to Weldon. There usually isn't much action right there at the ramp, so I normally wouldn't start fishing until I got to the I-95 bridge. Stay to the right as you go downstream. Once you go past the nice house that sits on the right side, just as you get to I-95, you are in good fishing water. Look for the "Happy Shad Roll" to tell you where the fish are. When shad are relaxed and in a place they like in the river, they will roll, splash, and generally make it known that they are about. Also look for osprey swooping down over the water. They like shad fishing too.

Equipment and Tackle

Let's assume you have found the fish—they are right there in front of you. You can see them swimming past you in the water; it is quite clear, and they are splashing in the pool. In this situation, fish with a light fly rod, generally a 4–5 weight, with a floating line. I like a brightly colored streamer with a weighted head, tied on a size 4–6 freshwater streamer hook. A Clouser Minnow also works.

Keep the fly above the heads of the fish. If it goes beneath them, they will move away from it. Anything that goes above them will get a look. You will actually see the reaction of the shad as your fly goes by them. Some will rise up for an instant and go down; others will give chase and turn away. Then one will come right up and slash at

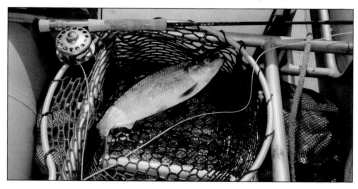

Floating line on a 6-weight rod fooled this fish.

it, often missing. When they don't, you find out shad are great fighters. The bigger ones, those approaching 18 inches or more, will leap like tarpon.

Some Areas Demand Caution

On down the river, there are a couple places demanding caution. If you are a good canoeist, kayaker, or rafter, then you know what to do and don't need my help. If not, you should pull up to the bank and check ahead when you see a drop-off, then decide whether you want to run it or portage around it. Keep your gear light for just such an occasion. I recommend that you do not try to run the rocks at Weldon under any circumstance, no matter what your experience. Pull out at the US-301 highway bridge. You need two cars for this, by the way, in case you haven't figured that out yet.

One other place that warrants special consideration is the area known as "The Gap." Large boulder formations on either side of the river form, well, a gap. The river takes a big turn to the right through a pretty narrow chute here. It would be wise to check it out ahead of time if you have not run it previously. It's a good place to portage with a canoe or kayak. Let me add that all of this fishing is done when the water on the river is running low. Oftentimes during shad season they hold the water back at the dam. That is what we are talking about here. If motorboats are able to run upstream from Weldon, then do not attempt to fish up there in a canoe or kayak because there's too much water, moving too fast. Check the water data for the Gaston Dam on the Internet; if it's low, it's probably safe to try.

Other than that, the river is pretty mild, flowing through very nice country where you can spot eagles, osprey, deer, turkey, and many different species of birds and ducks. As an occasion to fish for shad by the thousands in almost total seclusion, it is a trip that has definite rewards for the intrepid angler.

A Memorable Charter

Kids love shad fishing.

When I was guiding, I met up with my charter for the day at the boat ramp in Weldon. You have to shuttle when you do raft trips. Leave one vehicle at the take-out point, then load everybody into the tow vehicle and drive back upstream to launch. The father had never taken his two boys on a long fishing trip, so we were going to keep it under five hours. As soon as we launched the boat, it started, "Where are the fish Captain Gordon?" "Do you think we'll catch a lot of them Captain Gordon?" "Do you have any snacks Captain Gordon?" Their dad would just laugh from the other end of the raft as I patiently talked and goofed around with them. They were nice little dudes and we were having fun. I told them we'd have to get downstream a little

Some of these fish get pretty big.

way to find the fish. Until then, I entertained them with silly jokes and by pointing out the wildlife on the river. Safe to say, they were more amused by the idea of a goat that was living on an island than they were about the eagle that flew right over us.

But then we got to the fish. They could both cast, and as soon as we got to the fish, they were catching shad on their little spinning rods. Their father entertained himself by watching them while he caught shad after shad on his 5-weight fly rod and the size-six streamer fly I gave him. We got down to the take-out point, and the boys were talking the whole time. They caught fish for four solid hours, and I think they could have gone four more. It was a wonderful time and the father left a nice note thanking me for being so patient and kind with his kids. It's just what shad fishing is all about. There's no pressure, it's just fun.

Dams like these were built along the fall line of small rivers in the Carolinas for textile mills, and shad will concentrate at them.

Shad are available from the rivers feeding into Albemarle Sound in North Carolina to the St. John's River upstream of Jacksonville, Florida. Similar techniques will work wherever they are found. Sometimes you may need to fish a sinking fly line to get down closer to the fish. The same standards apply, and they will check out things that swing over their heads. Different colors work on different rivers. Pink is the go-to color on the Roanoke, while green gets it done in others. Ask around. If all else fails, tie a fly with three different colors on it and even fish two flies in tandem. If you get it just over their heads, they'll check it out. I once heard someone ask an older angler at a boat ramp why shad bite if they are not feeding. "Well," he said, "they don't got hands."

Chapter Four

Striped Bass

The absolute number-one place to catch a striped bass on a fly in the Southeast is the Roanoke River near Roanoke Rapids, North Carolina, just off I-95. Other rivers host stripers, including the Neuse and Cape Fear in North Carolina, Savannah in

A typical Roanoke striper.

Georgia, and St. John's in Florida. But none match the sheer numbers of fish in the Roanoke. During the spring spawning run from the last weeks of April through the first weeks of May, catching a striper is as close to a sure thing as there is in fishing anywhere around the world. The Roanoke hosts the third-largest spawning population of stripers on the East Coast in a river that is miniscule in comparison to the Hudson or the Chesapeake Bay. That's a load of fish in a small space. It's not impossible to catch a hundred fish in the 3- to 5-pound range range in a day. There are also some monsters; I've seen plenty over 30 inches on fly.

Roanoke River Trip

We launched the boat in the dark. There was a light at the ramp so it wasn't as scary as it sounds, and there was a moon so I could see down river as I left the dock. As I gunned the boat up on plane, I saw wakes of stripers as they shied away from us. I wanted to put as much distance as I could between us and the boat ramp before the rest of the crowd launched. After about ten minutes, I shut down and put out the electric motor.

"Cast to the bank," I said to my buddies, Derek and John. They had arrived at my trailer in Weldon at 4:00 A.M. after a night of partying in Durham. My alarm clock was going off as they walked in the door. Now they were shaking off cobwebs as they limbered up their casting arms. I had both of them casting handmade diving flies on intermediate line. The flies were bright white so they could be seen in the murky water. They both cast and stripped their flies several times. "Now let them pause a second so the fly suspends in the water." They did and were both immediately rewarded with strikes from 4-pound stripers. If I say to you that we had fish or strikes on every cast for the next three hours with not another boat in sight, that will

Eight-pound fish brought up from the bottom with a sinking line.

sound like hyperbole typically associated with bad outdoor writing so I won't say it, but that's what happened!

Most fly-rod fish on the Roanoke are caught on fast-sinking fly lines loaded onto 8-weight rods. Use a short 3- to 4-foot leader of 10- to 15-pound monofilament so the fly is close to the end of the line, on the bottom. Make a long cast. If you use a 350-grain fly line from one of the major manufacturers, it will list a sink rate in ips (inches per second). Count down to assure that it's getting deep. Most of the time, fifteen to twenty-five seconds will be enough, then start a retrieve of hard strips about a foot long. The strikes will be jarring, and when it's good you'll get a fish on, a strike, or a follow on almost every cast.

I was among a group of fly-fishing guides who pioneered this fishery in the mid-1990s. We figured out that using a boat equipped with a trolling motor set on the lowest speed enabled us to keep the bow pointed into the current. That way both anglers could cast their lines across the current so their flies could be presented broadside right down the middle of the river. This would often out-produce the number of strikes by guys fishing jigs, and sometimes even those using bait.

High-Water Technique

On one charter, high-water levels were making the striped bass fishing difficult for most people on the Roanoke. Fish were scattered all over, and it was so deep from an extremely rainy winter that it was difficult to get a fly down to them. I had figured out that by getting in behind log jams off the main current, I could find concentrations of fish. This particular morning I had a young couple with me from Charleston, South Carolina. The husband had shallow-water

People tend to get happy when they catch their first fish on fly.

experience, but his wife, Annie, had never caught a fish on a fly rod. I showed them how to cast the heavy lines. "Slow down your casting stroke. Stop your forward motion lower than you normally would, so you will have a bigger loop. This will keep your line from getting fouled."

The guy picked it up quickly due to his previous experience, but Annie was having some trouble. When you find the fish on the Roanoke, you really find the fish. He was hooking up on every cast. After working with her about fifteen minutes, she was punching out 60-foot casts. I showed her how to retrieve line with her rod tip close to the water to eliminate slack. Suddenly, she stopped in the middle of a strip coming tight to a nice fish. The New Year's Eve Ball doesn't light up as brightly as her face did. Catching your first fish on a fly rod will do that to you. By the end of the trip, both of their arms were sore from catching nice stripers all day.

Top-Water Technique

The most exciting way to target striped bass is with top-water flies, but it requires dedication. You need to be first on the water in the morning. That means launching your boat before 5:00 A.M. and getting downstream around the first few bends before anybody else is fishing. You will actually see the fish on the top of the water as they move around. Throw a popper—any popper—and it will probably get smacked. This fishing is great with a 6-weight fly matched to a floating line. Use a tapered leader with a tippet of at least 12-pound test so you can get the fish in quickly without tiring it out. Sometimes you will get multiple strikes on the same cast.

One night I opened my fly box looking for just the right thing for the morning top-water action. I had one small popper that

Topwater is the way.

looked more appropriate for bass fishing than striper fishing, but something about it spoke to me. The next morning I dropped it next to a big rock downstream from the boat ramp. A big swirl came up under it, sucking down the little popper. I knew something was up when the fish ran upstream, taking line. Most of the fish on the Roanoke that are less than 5 pounds can be brought to hand just by stripping in the line. I now had this fish on the reel and it was still running. It ended up being close to 12 pounds, which is not a huge striper, but a nice one for this river, and the best one the Roanoke ever gave me.

More Roanoke Techniques

The Roanoke fishery in recent years has not matched what it was when I was guiding there in the 1990s, but it's still pretty much fun if you haven't fished it. Any small fishing boat will work. You can sometimes fish right at the ramp with a canoe or kayak and be into fish all day. Bass boats, johnboats, and small center consoles are the most prevalent because they allow you to run down river to find

Get out early.

a less crowded spot. Let me add a word of caution: Forget going upriver from the ramp at Weldon even if the water is high and other fishermen are headed that way. You don't know where those rocks are lurking a foot below the surface! There's your warning; now you're on your own.

These techniques should apply on any river in the Southeast where striped bass are present. If they are deep, go after them with a sinking line. If the water is getting a bit warmer, try the top-water bite. Remember that early and late are better, with the sinking line as the way to go after the sun rises a bit. If that doesn't work, a diving fly fished on an intermediate line will sometimes get responses when nothing else will.

A classic morning on a southeastern coastal river.

These are hard-hitting fish and pull hard. If you keep a couple, remember that the striped bass is in some trouble everywhere they swim these days. Don't kill more than you're going to eat today. The glory days of striped bass fishing may be behind us, but hopefully we can keep them going into the future.

Chapter Five

Redfish

The entrance to a redfish paradise.

The old timers in North Carolina call them puppy drum or red drum. It's spottail bass in South Carolina, red bass in North Florida. Whatever you call them, when you fly fish for reds in southern low-country areas, the first thing to understand is that the water is not gin clear like you see on the television shows.

Knowing the tides is the difference between success and failure.

You won't be able to see the bottom much of the time. Recognize too, if you just flail along the banks the same way you would blind cast with a spinning rod, you are going to be disappointed. You must fish where you can see them, which means understanding tides and what they do to the water where the reds live.

It's All about Shallow Water

Let's say you want to catch a redfish on a fly. The best way to do this is by hiring a guide. You call up the one you saw on a television show. That seems smart enough because he has lots of pictures on his website of people holding redfish. He must be good, right? He takes you out in his bay boat, blasting across the river to what must be his secret spot. He drops down his trolling motor and instructs you to cast to the bank. So you cast. And you cast. And you cast. You do not catch a redfish. You catch a small speckled trout and a flounder, which he says is a great day.

First, any water around here that's deep enough to run a trolling motor is too deep to be fly fishing for redfish. If you can't see the bottom, you can't see the fish. If you can't see the fish, you aren't catching any either. That's not to say you will never catch a redfish by blind casting with a fly rod because it happens. I've done it myself, but not often and not with any other idea than just doing something for a little while until the tide moves.

TIDES CREATE THE PERFECT WATER DEPTH

To catch a redfish on a fly in the low country from North Carolina to North Florida, you must fish one of two tides, either a negative low or an extreme high. What's a negative low you ask? Find the week around the full moon for this month. Then look at the low tides, probably in the mornings. There should be a number next to the time. That number represents the amount of water there will be at the peak (high) or nadir (low) of that tide. Suitable smartphone apps to determine tides are listed in Appendix VI.

If there is a negative sign next to the low tide, that is a negative low. When that occurs, the water will be so low that there are only a few places for the fish to hold. The water there will be so shallow

Fish the negative lows and the extreme highs for reds.

that when the fish move around to feed, you'll be able to see them. That of course presupposes there will be redfish in the place you look.

Remember, I also said an extreme high; that probably seems counterintuitive. But the high-tide fishing presents a different set of fishing circumstances entirely, which has become legendary since it was pioneered in South Carolina. The extreme high water will allow the redfish access to the fiddler crab flats on top of the spartina marshes that exist on either side of a creek or river. This occurs

Redfish candy.

There are a lot of them!

from Beaufort, North Carolina, down to Jacksonville, Florida. Look at the areas behind the creek banks. There will be very tall grass on the edge, but behind there will be short grass. It weaves together to create a firm bottom that the small, quarter-sized crabs can't disappear into, and there are a lot of crabs.

When the conditions are prime and the water gets deep enough, which happens about six to ten days per month from spring through early fall, the reds will belly up to this crab buffet. This is the famous "tailing redfish" that fly anglers talk about. Tails and backs will be exposed, allowing you to see the fish as they swim and feed. It is extremely visual, very addicting, and heart pounding, causing anglers to make plans months in advance.

Coastal wild animals instinctively know how to use the tides.

The Right Boat

You may have surmised by now that you can't hunt redfish in just any kind of boat. A standard center-console bay boat draws too much water to fish at low tide, while at high tide you are limited to wadeable areas near where you anchor the boat. Also, some flats aren't hard but covered with "puff mud," soft layers of muck that can grab you tighter than a kid with a popsicle. If you wade, watch out for gray, grassless spots and test questionable areas. It smells really awful too. Ask my wife what my wading shoes smell like in the back of my truck.

A canoe or kayak draws the right amount of water, but you are limited to marshes near the access area where you launch. Your fishing window is short so you want to maximize your time. The best boat is what's known as a "poling skiff." It's a small, lightweight boat with a mostly flat bottom, a platform over the engine at the stern, and a push pole that is used to propel the boat silently toward the fish.

A perfect poling skiff for getting shallow.

Notice I did not say a "flat-bottom" boat. The popular skiff of the Carolinas makes too much noise that spooks the fish the first time the water smacks off the gunwale. A well-designed poling skiff moves swiftly, surely, and almost silently when poled in the shallows. It allows you to creep within casting range, sometimes so close the fish are under your feet while you gape down at them.

Tackle for Redfish

An 8-weight fly rod is the best choice. It allows you to cast the buggy, leggy flies that redfish seem to like, and it also has the power to beat the wind on breezy summer evenings. A substantial reel with a sealed drag capable of holding around 100 yards of 30-pound dacron backing is necessary because a hooked red will zoom off heading for deep water. A good drag helps slow down, then turn the fish. A floating line is the obvious choice for the very shallow water conditions. Generally, a 9-foot tapered leader ending in 12-pound tippet will work, but if the fish are spooky, I'll go to a 12-foot leader.

Any fly that looks like a shrimp or a crab will most likely get bitten if presented correctly. Make sure, however, that you take your

Buggy-looking flies in bright colors work well to imitate shrimp in off-colored water.

conditions into account. If fishing the low tides, the water will be murky, making it hard for the fish to see your offering. Pink, orange, and bright green are good fly-color choices. To make the hook ride point up, I often use a bend back–style tie. Some guides like flies with lead eyes, which also turn the hook up.

On the flats where the spartina sticks up 6 to 24 inches above the water, a weedless fly keeps it from hanging up on the retrieve. I have experimented a good deal and found that the double-post mono weed guard is the best choice. Lately, I have been tying on hooks normally used by freshwater bass anglers to fish plastic worms. They ride hook point up and the bend near the hook eye acts as a weed guard without deflecting strikes from fish.

Finding Fishy Locations

To locate flats and lots of spartina creeks, use online mapping and satellite photo apps. That is where you will find the fish. Check tide

The things fly fisherman dream about.

charts to find the highest and lowest tides during summer months. Determine areas that may be right for fly fishing by watching where the tournament anglers and gear fishermen go to catch redfish. Sometimes the best tailing flats are located adjacent to the same spot where a redfish pro won the last tournament. Conversely, if you go out at low tide, you may be all alone in the same spot that is shared by three boats at high tide. Then you can see those fish busting shrimp in 4 inches of water that the bay boat guys never see.

Red fishing with a fly rod is not a numbers game. Yes, you may find a school penned up in a creek somewhere and catch a dozen or more. That happens, but not a lot. Mostly it's a game of one here and another there. Lure anglers and bait guys won't understand what you're so excited about when you tell them about the "tailer" you saw on the grass flat that took a small shrimp fly. They'll ask how many you caught. You'll say that was the only one and they will look at you funny. It's all good. Fly fishing is about the how, not the how many.

A Fish Tale

It's high tide in the marshy creeks along the North Carolina coast. Sciae (*Sciaenops ocellatus*), the red drum, is in the deep water of the channels that flow through the marshes. Here she can swim easily, prowling for shrimp, crabs, and minnows. When the water gets high enough, she will leave the channels for the flats where fiddler crabs dig a thousand holes in the mud. These flats provide protection for the crabs at low tide and food in the form of the microscopic organisms they eat. Sciae could not access the flats just an hour or two earlier.

There is no water there three hours before and after the top of the tide. Other forms of life join her on the flats: finger-sized mullet, peanut menhaden, blue crabs, fiddler crabs, shrimp.

At high tide, this is what it looks like.

As the water floods the flat, Sciae glides silently between the stalks of high grass along the creek channel. She's over 30 inches long and almost 15 pounds, yet the grass stalks barely part when she swims by. To an observer, it might have been a breeze, not a big fish, which moved the grass. She crosses onto the flat, immediately on alert. Shadows. Splashes. Unnatural sounds. She doesn't have many enemies here, the water is too shallow for them. When she was younger, though, she had a close call with an osprey that swooped down on her but missed by just enough. She still bears a scar. Birds aren't big enough to be a problem anymore. Still, she knows anything over her head is a potential enemy.

An angler on the front deck of a skiff scans the grass flats. He and his friend like to fish for reds with fly rods. Fishing in this shallow, weed-choked water is difficult. The cast needs to be dead on target because all the advantages are with the fish. That is why they do it; the challenge. They release any fish they catch.

IN JUST INCHES OF WATER

As she moves along the flat, Sciae instinctively slides into the shallowest water near the shoreline. This gives her the advantage. Her prey has a difficult time escaping because there is simply no place to go. Sciae spots a fiddler crab straying too far from its hole. The crab is in the open, feeding. She effortlessly quickens her pace. The fiddler tries to disappear down a hole. Sciae tilts her head down, flares her gills and opens her mouth. This creates a powerful vacuum that whisks the crab into her mouth. It is immediately thrown into the crusher plates at the back of her throat and quickly smashed into easily digestible bits. It can't even begin to mount a defense.

When the redfish eats the fiddler crab, she is only in 5 inches of water. Her tail stands straight up in the air and it splashes on the surface. Both anglers hear it. The angler in the front of the skiff grabs his fly rod and eases into the water gingerly. Any excess noise will spook her. Carefully, quietly, he wades toward the redfish feeding on the grassy shoreline.

Sciae continues to cruise down the bank. There is another crab out in the open. With a short burst from her tail, she easily nails it. The angler sees the splash as the redfish accelerates. The same movement the fish makes to feed shows the angler where it is. He continues to stalk. Sciae feels good now. Confident. She moves up the grass to even shallower water, 4 inches deep. Many crabs have their holes here, easy pickings. She glides along. Her flank skims dry ground, dorsal fin flat on her back. She is almost invisible from the surface except for a small hump.

SIXTY FEET AWAY, NO ROOM FOR ERROR

The angler eyes the hump of her back and the tip of her tail fin. He is in position, preparing to cast. His fly is a perfect imitation of a small crab. He needs to get it directly in her path and make a soft landing. It's a 60-foot cast with no room for error. Don't let her see the fly line in the air. Don't slap the surface. Don't drag the line across her back. Lots of don'ts.

There is a small splash up ahead. Sciae moves over to investigate. A crab just under the surface. Barely moving. Struggling in the grass. A very easy mark. She moves in. Flares her gills. Opens her mouth. It's gone.

The angler reacts perfectly. A strip set. He puts the fly right into the corner of her mouth before she can get it inside her crushers.

The rewards are there for a skilled angler.

Sciae knows something is wrong. Her prey has jabbed her in the side of the mouth and is pulling on her. Powerful sweeps of her tail get her off the flat. She feels safe in the deep water but she slowly tires and is pulled inexorably to the surface.

The anglers land the big red gently, almost reverently. They know this is a special fish. They get the hook out, place her in the water, take several photos, then watch as the redfish speeds away. She leaves a large wake, like a torpedo moving through the water.

They only come in this shallow to feed.

In the safety of the deep water in the creek channel, Sciae slows down. The danger has passed. That crab was unfamiliar and its image will be retained. She won't use that feeding flat anymore. She is almost too big to be in such shallow water anyway. When the weather cools, she will move out of the creeks and into the open ocean to join hundreds of other fish of her age.

MORE DANGER AHEAD

There will be more danger that she doesn't even know—sharks, dolphin, other fishermen, menhaden netters. She will continue to grow until she is very big, and very old. Potentially, she could reach 50 or 60 pounds and live thirty years or more. Her greatest function will be to produce offspring. Her body will manufacture more than 3 million eggs when she spawns.

The anglers stalk the flats until the tide reaches its peak. They catch two more reds, but neither approaches the size of the first one. A great day! Neither angler will forget the sight of that first big fish in water that shallow. The motor of the skiff starts on the first try and the sound of the outboard shatters the silence. A flock of ibis flush at the sound. After a few minutes, stillness returns to the marsh. Other crabs crawl through the mud to feed. Other red drum swim in the creek channels.

All or Nothing in Winter

If you want to catch a lot of redfish on a fly but with the risk of a skunk, the best time to do it is in winter. The fish gather into big schools at this time of year. The only problem is that they gather into big schools. If you can't find the school, you won't find anything at all. There are a few places near my home that host winter redfish schools. Let me see if I can put the pieces together for you.

A perfectly clear winter morning for Chris Ellis.

HUNDREDS OR THOUSANDS

The areas where schools of redfish gather in winter are all creeks off of larger bays. They all have wider areas inside them that have open flats. This is important because on sunny days in winter these flats warm up first and the fish become active on them. The right flats will host schools with numbers in the hundreds or even thousands of redfish. These creeks also have deeper holes on bends that are near these flats. Fish will use these as primary feeding areas on less sunny days. If you find one of these holes, it will be possible to catch dozens of fish without moving your boat. When it's right, it's spectacular.

I pulled into the creek on a blustery day in January. This creek was the only area that I could get to without getting soaked on the open water, which was not an option when it was 45°F. That was fine though, because this particular creek was exactly where I would have gone anyway. There are usually redfish in it all year using one area or another, and it had a deep spot next to an oyster bar with easy access to a big flat. It's prime winter fishing territory.

The tide had just passed high and was now going out. I anchored downtide of the hole I wanted to fish. I had on a small weighted streamer with a floating fly line on my 6-weight rod. I made a long cast right where the oyster bar ends and the deeper water begins. Now when I say deeper water, I mean it's about 6 feet deep at high tide. As my fly was washed toward me with the current, I stripped my line in just fast enough to jump it a little and keep the line tight. On the third cast it got a lot tighter and I was hooked up with a 6-pound redfish. This was the mother lode. The fish were stacked up. I caught them for two solid hours. Included in the mix was a 30-incher and a 4-pound speckled trout. That's what can happen when redfish get stacked up in a hole in the winter.

JUMPING SHRIMP ARE A SIGN

The same creek has a nice flat. I went back with a friend a week later. It was a calm, clear, beautiful winter day. Highs were going to be near 60°F and the sun was shining. I knew the same fish I had caught a week earlier would be using the flat. I started poling with Chris on the bow. As I scanned the water in front of us, I saw some shrimp skipping on the surface and a back out of the water. I turned the skiff with the push pole so I could line up a good cast off of his left shoulder.

There is a redfish in this picture.

"Look at 10 o'clock. Shrimp jumpin', 80 feet." He lined up his rod and made a perfect cast that landed his small shrimp fly just to the left of where I had seen the jumps. He started stripping in erratic motions to mimic a swimming shrimp. They usually make a couple of jumps in the water, then a pause, then several more jumps. His line got tight and he was hooked up to a 5-pounder while I shot a video. There were more and I was able to keep us out of the school by back-poling a little bit.

The fish in the water looked like moving blobs, roughly fish-shaped. Sometimes I could see a flash of white from their bellies or when they opened their mouths to eat. The shrimp were still jumping too and sometimes a few gulls would hover over them as well. It was definitely a good day made possible by having all the pieces of a perfect winter redfish creek, combined with perfect winter fishing conditions. Perfection doesn't happen too often, but when it does, be prepared.

A perfect end.

I told you they like to get in the grass.

Their colors really stand out when the sun hits them just right.

Chapter Six

Bluefish

The first saltwater fish that most people catch is probably a bluefish. They are around every inlet and beachfront from New Jersey to Florida, from April to November, and are almost impossible to escape at times, especially if you are looking for bigger game and the 6-inchers move in. Most of the blues we catch where I live in North Carolina will be less than 2 pounds, with a vast majority

First bluefish for young Emerson.

of those less than 12 inches. On a light rod, however, and with the right attitude, they are a fun way to learn about fly presentation and casting to breaking fish.

Chasing Blues from the Beach

The point of land at the end of a barrier island leading into an inlet can be a great place to find all kinds of fish in the summer. It's best to fish on foot with an outgoing tide. Position yourself on the downcurrent side of any rip or current line that forms on the outward side of the inlet. If there are baitfish there, the game fish will follow. Use a 6-weight rod with an intermediate line and let the current sweep your fly out. Retrieve it in the back eddy that forms.

Derek Brock is working a rip with a back eddy in an inlet.

That's what I was doing when the blues almost took off my toes! They came in a wave that was chopping everything smaller than their 12-inch size. I had to jump out of the water to make sure they didn't mistake my toes for the little silversides they were after. Blues

Watch the birds, they'll tell you what's going on.

have very sharp teeth that can easily draw blood. But then I had fun catching them one after another for the next hour.

If I said you could reliably target bluefish over 10 pounds or even over 5 pounds in waters from North Carolina to Florida, I would be lying. If anybody tells you that, they are lying. It just doesn't happen with any sort of regularity. Do people catch bluefish over 10 pounds? Yes they do, occasionally. I've done it myself, but to say, "Today I will fish for blues over 10 pounds," is foolish. It's a happy accident that occurs just by being on the water the day they come through.

Gear and Tackle

Can you have fun catching small bluefish? You should! Start with a light fly rod, generally a 6-weight. That's about as light as you'll want to go because the wind makes it more difficult to cast a lighter rod. If you have a 4- or 5-weight trout rod that you want to try out on 12-inch bluefish, go for it. It might work in calmer conditions. A floating line is usually all that is needed but an intermediate is nice for getting below surface currents when beach or inlet fishing.

Normally these fish eat small baitfish—silversides and small anchovies less than 2 inches long. Any small streamer like a Clouser or synthetic fiber pattern will work. They don't even have to be accurate replicas of the minnow being copied. In fact, one of my favorite things to say to somebody who has just tied a fly that is sloppy or poorly tied is, "I'm pretty sure a bluefish would eat that." There is truth in that since they are quite aggressive, not because the fly is all that great. Only say that to a good friend because people get mad at you when they figure out what you meant by that comment. I also like to use small poppers, but they don't last very long. As I am sure you know, the bluefish is famous for its teeth. They will shred fingers,

They call them choppers for a reason. Look at the size of the mouth and teeth.

flies, and leaders quickly. Use a 40-pound monofilament bite tippet attached to your shock tippet with a surgeon's knot.

If you have a boat, simply go to the nearest inlet and look for birds diving or some bait on the surface; those signs will normally mean fish. Get your boat into position around the birds. Look at the water. There will be splashes where the birds hit the water, picking off minnows. What you want are splashes coming up from the water, caused by the fish.

Birds on the water mean fish underneath.

If you don't have a boat, the best place to start is the beach near the inlet. Even better is if there is a rock pile or jetty of some sort there. Consult your charts for an outgoing tide, which is usually best. If you have a smartphone (of course you do), there are numerous tide apps. The one I prefer and have been using for years is called

"AyeTides." I don't mind giving them a recommendation because it's been so useful to me over the years. It's the second-most-expensive piece of software I have ever purchased for a smartphone but worth every penny.

These apps help determine fishing conditions.

First Fish

It was a perfect October day. The wind was light from the northwest, which blows straight over the dune tops here. My little boat was skimming over the water's surface as my son, Will, and I scooted out the inlet. There was a friendly school of bluefish working on top, just off the beach several hundred yards. My goal was to get Will to catch his first fish.

I shut down the engine about 100 feet away, grabbing a light rod perfect for catching small bluefish. This was a spinning rod day. Will was only three at the time. He made a short cast with a metal jig and started reeling it in. It took about three seconds before he had a fish on. He laughed with delight as the little scrapper put up a good

This kid is over 6' 3" now.

fight. I can still hear those laughs today as I look at his 6-foot 4-inch, athletic frame and remember that day with the little guy sitting on my lap holding his first fish. If you have never caught a saltwater fish on a fly, then go out and catch a bluefish before you try anything else. It will help you put all the rest of the pieces together.

They call them yellow-eyed devils. I wonder why?

Chapter Seven

Speckled Trout

Fall means speckled trout.

Fall in North Carolina means many things to people, from football games to fishing and hunting. For anglers, fall brings the best fishing of the year. One of the fish species that really puts on a show in October and November is the speckled trout. After a long summer of being in small groups or singles in marshes and rivers, speckled trout seek out company and move en masse toward their wintering areas. As they do this, they feed with abandon. If you find a spot that is holding a school of trout on the move in October, you may catch more fish in a few hours than you did all year.

> The bigger fish will be in back eddies along the shoreline. Keep your fly along the edge for as long as you can. Hits can come at any time.

I hit one of my favorite marsh spots in October. I anchored the boat on the edge of a flat next to a drop-off. There was a hole next to the marsh grass where the current swept in a back eddy on the incoming tide. Before I even made the first cast, I saw speckled trout smacking shrimp along the grass edge. Using a slightly weighted shrimp fly and a 6-weight intermediate line, I was into fish immediately. These were not monsters; most fish were barely keeper-sized, but I did manage to catch several nice ones.

Technique

The bite lasted as long as the tide kept moving. At one point I was merely making short casts and holding my rod tip low to the water without manipulating the fly at all. They were snapping at it like piranha. When speckled trout feed they don't take off after they grab something. You don't feel a huge tug. It's generally a tap or often just a tightening of the fly line. Videos of feeding specks will show them grabbing minnows so quickly that you literally can't see them moving. After they get the snack, they just stop and wait for the next one. If you don't react when you feel that little tap, you miss them. Keep your rod tip almost in the water so your line stays straight. That sag that develops between the tip and the water when you have your rod up a little will keep you from feeling strikes. Even the bigger speckled trout I've caught barely registered when they struck. Only when you set the hook do you realize you've gotten into a nice one.

So it was when I felt another tap. I stripped my line to set the hook but I didn't feel the wiggle of a 2-pound fish. I felt a thump. The bigger trout shake their heads when hooked while the smaller ones wiggle so you know right away. This one wanted to run too. I let it. When it was done, all my fly line was off the reel and I could feel the big thumps out there. It felt good and solid. When it rolled boatside, I legitimately thought it was a small tarpon since it was so silver and much bigger than I expected. It was the biggest speckled trout I'd ever caught, 7¼ pounds. That's pretty big around here. Because of a camera malfunction, I have no photos of this fish, which seems to always happen with trophy-sized fish. All I have are my memories, which often have to suffice.

The cool thing about fall speckled trout fishing is that this is one of the times that we as fly anglers can catch as many, and often more, fish than the gear anglers, which is pretty amazing. There are times when I have been at the Cape Lookout Rock Jetty that usually draws eighty boats on the weekend and been catching a trout on every cast, while other guys around me casting jigs or plugs struggled to get

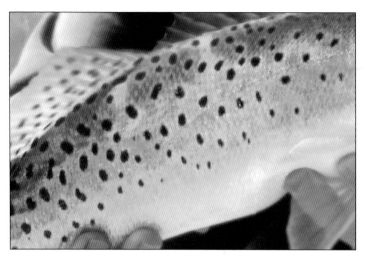

Some say the speckled trout is the prettiest fish that you will catch inshore.

bites. Of course, other times the roles have been reversed, but that's not really why we're here now is it?

Where Trout Hide

Let's talk about maximizing our chances with speckled trout. Look for a washout hole in a tidal marsh with some good current running through it. Now find that one spot where the creek narrows down between two sand or oyster bars or where a bar runs near the creek bank. Basically, it's any place where the water is funneled into a smaller space.

Rock piles like jetties or break walls are great spots to find fish closer to the ocean or in the ocean. Look for deep sloughs just off the surf line. Any place that funnels current will gather baitfish so that is where you want to spend your time. Cast a size-2 Clouser Minnow on an intermediate line with a 6–8 weight fly rod and there is a good

A typical marsh creek at low tide: The deeper water is to the left. Fish from the shallow side to the deeper side.

chance you will get bitten by a trout during the months of October and November.

FLIES WORKED THIS DAY

I was in the boat, running out the inlet to a spot noted for producing lots of late-fall and early winter speckled trout. I pulled up to the rocks then dropped anchor close enough to reach the rocks but far enough away to avoid spooking the fish. I was casting a small minnow fly in red over white with an intermediate line in about 8 feet of water. It landed perfectly, just short of the rocks. I let it swing with the current then stripped it off the bottom with a soft snap of my line hand. The current did most of the work. When I felt

For some reason they like red.

something slightly different, I strip-set, putting the hook into a thump—a speckled trout about 3 pounds. After I got the thump to the boat, I realized that I had forgotten the landing net. Slipped my hand under the fish and swung it in the boat in one smooth motion. Nice. This fish was going to be released into the frying pan! I cast again, let it sink, stripped the line, and felt the strike. Set! Thump! Excellent!

After six casts and as many fish, other people fishing nearby began to take notice. This is a pretty popular place to fish so there's always somebody there, especially in early winter. A friend of mine pulled in nearby, so we began talking back and forth between the boats.

"Whatya gettinum on?"

"Size 2 red over white Clouser."

There were nods of affirmation. I pulled another fish over the side but nothing for the other guy. Sounds of muted conversation mixed with the sound of gear bags being zipped open and tackle trays being rifled.

"Okay, I got something that should work now."

Another fish for me.

"Damn! You tearin' it up."

I cast it out in pretty much the same spot. The line came tight almost immediately and I had another speck.

"Well hell, he's killin' 'em on that fly rod!"

I tried not to act like I was really enjoying myself while releasing the fish I was catching after I got my four. I wanted to let them go to see the looks on the guys' faces. After I had enough I said, "See y'all around." Then I fired up the motor and headed in.

Winter Hiding Places

Later in the winter, the speckled trout will move into creeks off the Intracoastal Waterway looking for deeper holes to survive the winter. The colder it gets, the better the chance of there being large numbers of fish in these little creeks. Speckled trout will move further up these creeks as it gets colder. On the days when the fingers of your casting hand feel like they have needles in them, the speckled trout might be in creeks so narrow you could jump across them. Well, maybe twenty years ago I could have. These fish will bite too.

WHAT TO USE

I like a 6-weight rod with an intermediate line and a 9-foot leader. You might want to have a 250-grain sinking line if there are some spots over 12 feet deep, while a floater is good if you find some really shallow spots worth checking. Ideally, the fly should hover or suspend in the water. There's something about a fly just hanging there they can't stand. The take will be subtle. That time when you felt like you might have been fouled on a piece of grass or something? It was probably a trout. Here's the real kicker: these might be the biggest speckled trout you get a chance to fool. The largest trout of the year are caught in these winter creeks. As a bonus, these areas can often be easily accessed by canoes, kayaks, or other cartop boats.

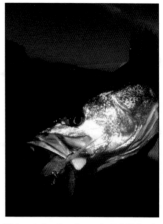

This winter trout wanted it fished slow and low.

Checking your map apps will often show a small creek upstream of a larger body of water. If that larger body of water is known as a good speck area, that little creek will hold fish when it gets cold. Most of these creeks only have gar and bowfin during the rest of the year. Find a spot where a road crosses over the creek; chances are there will be a place where a kayak can be easily dropped in. Many times the local folks will fish these spots. That's even better because then you really know it's worth trying. You can paddle along in the kayak and cast to the bend holes and long straightaways with streamers and have a real chance at catching a big speckled trout. As long as there is not a real hard freeze mixed with wintry precipitation, the fishing can be good all winter from the creeks west of Pamlico Sound in North Carolina all the way down through Georgia.

When I went under the bridge to get into the narrow section where we knew the trout wintered over, there was a skim of ice.

I slowly motored my little skiff through and upstream. The Weather Dude said it was going to be "sunny with highs in the 50s," but it sure didn't feel like that now. At least the sun was out. That made it doable. I dropped my anchor and started casting at the first bend. It took me a few casts to get the stiffness out of my shoulder joints. On my first good cast, I felt a tap. When I came tight it was a lovely 3-pound speck. There

No two spots are quite the same.

is an old saying that if you are going to keep a fish for dinner that you should keep the first fish you catch, not the last one. The first one could be your last, so in the cooler it went. Later that night it was put into a hot skillet with a little butter, seared on both sides, and served with a ponzu reduction sauce. My wife loves it when I bring speckled trout home. I proceeded on down the creek and in the next couple hours managed to catch four more nice ones. Great fishing for January.

Dress appropriately and the trout will reward you when you find the right creek in winter.

Summer Trout Action Is Hit or Miss

Night fishing is the best way to catch trout in summer.

Summer speckled trout action on a fly can be hit or miss. Fish spread out and become tough to find. Night fishing is a pretty sure bet for fly rodders, however. When the temperature gets pretty uncomfortable in the middle of the day, you should think about going out in the middle of the night. Check out the ends of the docks in areas you fish. Look to see if anybody has a light that is mounted *under* the dock. If you take an early-morning, first-light trip, you'll see them because they'll still be on. Then check them at night.

Don't even launch your boat until after 10:00 P.M. It'll be pretty obvious if the trout are in the lights because you'll see feeding splashes and jumping bait. Have several different flies handy. What you'll normally see them hitting is either small minnows or shrimp. A lot of times I'll start out with a small white popper and just let it drift into the light cone. Other times a hyperrealistic shrimp fly is the ticket while sometimes a small, white streamer fly works well. The strikes are pretty visual. There is either a nice *pop* when they get it, or you'll see them dart out from the darkness. Once in a while you'll be surprised at the size of the fish you get, and sometimes you'll hook something that you never see.

My friends came down from New Yawk. The tide we wanted to fish for tailing redfish wasn't until late afternoon the next day, so I suggested that we go night fishing. We ran down the Intracoastal and pulled up to the dock with the bright green light suspended underneath. The sounds emanating from the water were surreal. On full moons during summer evenings, you can hear croakers croaking, shrimp clicking, and who knows what else is making weird noises down there. In a small boat these sounds reverberate through the hull louder than you'd imagine. It makes for a wonderfully cacophonous symphony to accompany the pursuit of speckled trout.

Somebody once told me I hold fish like I'm playing a chord on a guitar.

As soon as we came tight on the anchor, I could see and hear feeding fish. When a fish eats a shrimp off the surface, it makes an unmistakable *pop*. Using a shrimp fly, Tim dropped his first few casts short of the light. Then he threw one that landed about 5 feet up-current of the green glow. It was drifting down perfectly. I told him to mend his line just a smidge that made the fly jump a little. A speckled trout nailed it right then. It was a nice fish that measured out around 15 inches and was maybe 2 pounds. The fish was nothing spectacular, but still pretty fun, and it beat watching summer reruns on cable in a hotel room. Later I got a shot, but my cast went too deep and landed behind the light. As soon as the line got tight, I knew it was trouble. Something big took off and wove a tapestry between the dock pilings. It was over quickly; fish and fly were history.

Beach Fishing Can Be Frustrating

Beach fishing with a fly rod in our region is usually frustrating. Our beaches are pretty flat and most of the time there has been so much "renourishment" (which means dumping dredged sand from shipping channels on the beach to save the mansions) that a lot of the natural life that should be present is gone. Things like mole crabs, razor clams, surf clams, and shrimp will not be found in an area that has recently been "nourished."

Having said that, in the fall, usually around a full moon in October or November, large schools of specks will flood out the inlets moving to the ocean. You can fish for them in front of the beachfront mansions if you like, but it's difficult because the schools often stay about 100 feet off the shore. Light-action, 8- to 9-foot spinning rods rigged for long casts with small plugs make a killing. If you can find a beach slough that is close in on the days when they are coming through, you can have a blast catching one speck after the

Ideal surf conditions for speckled trout: the water stays clean and the angler stays dry.

other. The swell needs to be down and the wind at your back because your casts need to be straight away from the beach. It's not easy and doesn't happen often.

INLETS ARE A BETTER OPTION

A better option is to fish around or inside inlets on shorelines with deep water nearby. I like to think of funnels. Find a spot where the current goes through an area that's a little deeper than the areas around it. The water should still go all the way through, since dead ends aren't as good. It could be as simple as the channel between two islands where everything has to go. Or it could be as subtle as a deeper slough near the inlet that only shows at low tide. Obviously, if your inlet has a jetty or rock groin of some kind, those are great. Look for spots where locals will park and fish before or after work. Sometimes it will be obvious just because of the cars. Outgoing tide is preferable, and if there is bait present, so much the better.

Thanksgiving is a special night. Also, I went speck fishing that morning before I started cooking the turkey and mashing the potatoes. I put my waders on next to the truck and trudged out to the shoreline. I was the only person carrying a stripping basket along with my gear pack. The three other guys out there looked at my fly rod with curiosity. They don't see a bunch of fly rods on the beach. The tide was moving out pretty fast and I was able to get my fly to swing along the edge of the drop-off. I was fishing a beach near a

Thanksgiving speckled trout.

boat channel about a mile from the inlet, guessing the trout would be holding right where it goes from 3 feet to about 20. I guessed right.

On my third cast I connected with a nice fish; same on my fifth cast and then again on my sixth cast. Every fish was released, which was even more confusing to the other guys. I figured I had enough to do that afternoon when it came to food preparation. I didn't need to add fish filleting to that list. I walked back to my truck with the fish still biting. The other guys fishing out there didn't do nearly as well. It happens.

Chapter Eight

Spanish Mackerel

The sun was just breaking over the horizon as we ran out of Beaufort Inlet. Paul Vrablic and I were on an early morning inshore fishing expedition. It was a perfect day in mid-May. The water temperature was nudging the mid-70°F range so we were out to catch anything we could find off the beach. Our first stop during the outgoing tide was an artificial reef. Birds were diving, and feeding fish splashed the surface of the water. We were using sink-

There are many rewards for getting an early start to your fishing day.

ing lines with small streamer flies on size-4 hooks. In the deep, obstruction-free water, we both fished at the same time, hooking up on small bluefish simultaneously. After a few fish each, the tide slacked off and so did the bite. My next plan was to check the incoming tide for the first big Spanish mackerel of the year running the beach. We were off.

Blitzing Fish on a Glassy Sea

It was very calm on the ocean, almost glassy. I had the throttle open all the way. We flew. After a fifteen-minute run, we were amazed by what we saw: the surface water boiled with the splashes of feeding fish. Small glass minnows were leaping for their lives, only to be intercepted by sharp-eyed seagulls. I told Paul to get in the bow with his 6-weight fly rod. He had a floating line with a small popper tied to his leader. I got the boat into position as he cast into the melee and began to make the fly pop. A fish struck immediately. When he set the hook, I realized that what he had was not a Spanish, but a 10-pound king mackerel! Unfortunately, the 40-pound fluorocarbon leader couldn't withstand those sharp teeth. The fight was over quickly. In the ocean, surprises will happen.

Paul now had to rig a new shock tippet and the fish were still busting. I assumed the position on the forward casting deck and

When you see birds doing this, it's a pretty good bet that feeding fish are underneath.

quickly hooked up. My fish, a feisty 3-pound Spanish mackerel, ran out a little line, giving me a fun scrap. I decided to let this one go. Being careful of the needle-sharp teeth, I extracted the hook using long-nosed pliers, dropped the fish head first into the water, then watched it dart off at top speed. Meanwhile, Paul was back in the game and had a fish already. The action continued unabated until the tide came in and high water dispersed the fish. We had two solid hours of nonstop surface action on Spanish mackerel up to 4 pounds. You couldn't possibly have more fun!

Three Things to Know

When fly fishing for Spanish mackerel, you need to be aware of three things. First, and foremost, are those teeth, which are sharp and interlock. I have experienced worse bites from 12-inch Spanish mack-

See how this nice-sized Spanish mackerel nicked the 40-pound shock tippet?

erel than from 15-pound bluefish! They have a way of shaking their heads at just the right (wrong) time to slash you open.

Next, is the clear water that they prefer. This precludes using wire leaders. I prefer a shock tippet of 30-pound fluorocarbon connected to my leader with a double surgeon's knot. The fluorocarbon almost disappears in the water, so fish don't shy off. Wire leaders let them know something is not quite right.

Third, consider their choice of food. Usually small and shiny, their prey has only one way to get away: swim very fast! So, use small, shiny streamers and move them as fast as you can. When you think you are stripping fast enough, go a little faster. This means ripping the line through your stripping hand in long pulls, then doing it again and again before the fly has a chance to settle. If your arm gets tired, and the water is calm and clear, try a crease fly on a size-2 hook. You don't have to move it as fast, and the fish will often, but not always crease fly take it as it floats on the surface motionless.

When to Fish

The first Spanish mackerel will hit the beaches sometime at the end of April or beginning of May, earlier farther south and later farther north. But, fish don't have iPhone calendars to keep their appointments. In some years, they will blitz beaches in April and in others, not until almost June; 70°F seems to be their magic number.

The biggest macs of the year are caught right

Don't put your fingers in there!

before they disappear for the season. Spanish mackerel in the 6- to 7- pound range can provide excellent targets for fly rodders in water less than 10 feet deep around shoals and inlets. You can often look down in the water to see them swimming under the boat! This is prime time for a popper and I have hooked Spanish that looked more like kings as they sky in the shallows. It's a great way to bid goodbye to summer fishing, and these bigger macs are the last hurrah as they migrate south. It also heralds the beginning of fall fishing.

This youngster got this nice mack attack on the last of the late summer action before water temperatures dropped below 70°F.

Chapter Nine

Atlantic Bonito

I was heading out the inlet in the early light of a May morning in Beaufort, North Carolina, with my old friend, Dr. Bill, in his 24-foot center console. We were going to a near-shore artificial reef where the water temp was 65°F. Just a few days earlier I had been out there by myself, only catching small bluefish. Today, we were sure that our quarry of choice would be present. As Bill piloted the boat into position around the reef, it was immediately apparent that bluefish would not be a problem. We could see the torpedo shapes of Atlantic bonito as they rocketed out of the water in a feeding frenzy. I had the first shot and fired a size 1/0 minnow imitation into the melee and was rewarded with a strike as soon as my line came tight. The fish

Portrait of a bonito as a young fish.

shot out across the surface with my fly line in tow and my hook in its mouth. I worked it back to the boat after another, shorter run and some nice digging at the boat. Bill expertly grabbed it by its tail, flipping it into the cooler. This fish was going on ice for a sashimi and grill festival with my family when I got home that afternoon.

A Sure Sign of Spring

When the sou'westers of spring start to blow along the coast, there are many sure signs that the weather is changing for the better. Blossoms appear on trees, bees come out to take advantage of those blossoms, and young men's fancies turn to thoughts of love. If you want to know what the best and surest sign of spring is along the coast, I'd say it is the arrival of the bonito schools. These fish begin to show up in massive numbers along the coastlines of South and North Carolina during the first two weeks of April and provide exciting fishing well into May.

WHERE TO FIND THEM

The best place to get in on this action is at any of the artificial reefs or live bottom. Good areas are located off Little River, Lockwoods Folly, Masonboro, New River, and Beaufort Inlets. Run out at first light and head to the nearest wreck, reef, or rock. If the water temperature is 65- to 70°F, the fish will most likely be waiting for you. It really is a great way to break in your open-water fishing season.

There is often much confusion in identifying the small tunas that frequent our inshore waters. Basically there are two species: The little tunny (or more popularly known as false albacore) can be distinguished by its high dorsal fin, squiggly lines on its back (or dorsal vermiculation) and black spots near its pectoral fin. The bonito has a long, low dorsal fin, horizontal racing stripes along its side, and very prominent teeth. By looking at the two fish, you can see a fundamental difference in how they pursue their prey.

The albie has a large mouth with its teeth recessed, and is a gulping feeder. The bonito has a small mouth with prominent teeth and is a grasper. For albacore fishing you can use flies or lures that have a longer body. For bonito fishing, use long shank hooks on your streamers or you will often get short strikes. Even though the bonito has nice dental work, there is not much call for bite leaders of any kind since they do not bite down the way a mackerel or a bluefish does. In fact, the bonito is known to be leader shy, so heavy line or wire will greatly reduce the number of strikes you get.

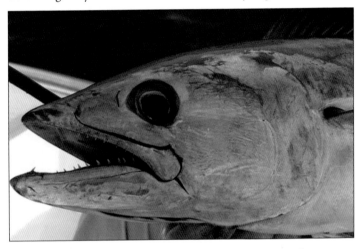

They have some nice teeth but don't bite through leaders very often.

How to Catch One

There are many ways to pursue bonito. I find, however, that the most fun and exciting way is to chase schools of breaking fish. This is classic surface action. You cast to them with an 8-weight fly rod, floating line, and any small- to medium-sized baitfish fly. Hook sizes from 2 to 1/0 in a gamut of colors, with pinks and greens working best. These fish are hungry, aggressive, and will hit almost anything. I've even caught them on Zara Spooks!

An easy-to-maneuver boat up to 24 feet that accelerates and slows quickly with room to walk around while fighting fish is ideal. Combined with the moderate southwest breezes we receive at this time of year, it is a great opportunity for small-boat anglers to get in on some action. If you have a fiberglass, flat-bottomed skiff of 18 feet or more, you are going to be okay. Something with a "V" bottom will serve you better because there is often a healthy chop running. Actually, if the weather is nice and there is a bit of breeze, the fishing is often better because the fish cannot see or hear the boat as well, and you will be able to get closer to them.

The inshore water temperatures reach 65°F sometime during April or early May, which is the time to start looking for bonito. They seem to like structure that breaks up current. When there is bait and water in their preferred temperature range, then the bones (as they are often referred to) will be over inshore reefs and wrecks. Check the fishing maps for sale at the tackle shops that will show the closest artificial reefs and wrecks to your preferred inlet.

WHEN THEY'RE DEEP

You won't always be able to cast to surface feeding fish. Often the schools of bonito will show on your depth finder so you can determine how deep they are. Then it is simply getting the fly down to the school where a bite is often not far behind. Use a 350-grain sinking line so you will be able to get down to them. Know the line's inches per second sink rate then count your line down to the approximate depth where the fish are holding before starting your retrieve. Here's

Bonito put a nice bend in an 8-weight.

an example: The fish are at 15 feet so that's 180 inches down. A 350-grain lines sinks about 8 inches per second so use your iPhone to divide 180 by 8 which translates into twenty-two seconds. But I'm not very good at math.

Make sure your reel can hold about 200 yards of backing with a drag surface up to the task of stopping a fish that can swim upwards of 30 miles per hour. A leader about 8 feet long with a 10-pound tippet is what I normally use. There are record-size fish here, so a big fish on a light tippet could put you in the books.

After you hook a bonito, your immediate reaction may be, "What's the big deal?" Don't be complacent. They tend to hesitate for a second before they put it in gear. If you are using a light tippet, make sure your fly line is clear and your drag set correctly or you will get snapped off in a hurry. The first run may be up to 100 yards or more, as the fish attempts to keep up with its buddies in the school.

When the bonito realizes it can't do this, it will sound, beginning a back-and-forth, see-saw type of battle that begrudges you every inch of line you gain back.

When it sees the boat, the dance will start all over. The second run will not be as far as the first but just about as fast. When the fish is finally ready to be landed, grab it right by the tail. Now is the tough part, deciding whether to keep it or put it back. You see, the Atlantic bonito is quite good to eat. If you decide to release it, get the hook out quickly and drop it head first into the water. If you want to keep the fish, however, you must get it on ice and bled out quickly. If the fish is taken care of properly on the boat, you will be pleased with the results later on. Cut a slit in the belly and in the gills up to the throat area and immerse completely in ice. They are great on the grill and amazing as sashimi.

Even Duke fans like to catch bonito.

First Speedster

My neighbor was a novice fly angler. The only fish he had caught on a fly in saltwater was a 6-inch bluefish two weeks earlier. This was going to be the day he got a bonito. The water was clear and calm and as the light came up with the dawn, so did the fish. I put him right on the fish and he proceeded to forget everything he ever knew about fly casting. He lost control of the line and couldn't make a cast. When he did make a cast, he shot the line on the back cast instead of the forward cast. It was a gorgeous 60-foot back cast. Unfortunately, the fish were 60 feet in front of us. He had to strip it back so he could cast again to the fish that were still busting in front of us. It didn't matter because there were so many fish that he hooked up almost immediately.

"I thought you told me I had to cast over there," he laughed. He got three nice runs from the almost 5-pounder. When the fish came alongside, I grabbed its tail, pulled the hook out and immersed it in ice. This was going to be the start of a great fish feast. When it was my turn, I used a top-water popper. In the calm water, they destroy poppers. I made an 80-foot cast over where I had just seen a fish break. When I started my retrieve, it was game on. First one, then another, then another bonito took a swing. The fourth strike finally got tight. That fish would join the other on ice. We ended up keeping two each and released a bunch more. It was a great introduction to more advanced fishing for my neighbor.

The Atlantic bonito is the best way I know to start spring ocean fishing. If you get the word that "the bonito are in," drop everything,

They look like somebody splashed paint near the tail.

head to the beach, and get after them. There is no better way to spend a spring morning than running out the inlet at first light then seeing fast-swimming fish fresh from the deep ocean blasting baitfish out of the water as the sun rises. I can't think of many things I'd rather be doing.

Chapter Ten

Cobia

If you want to catch a cobia on a fly rod, you have to fish for cobia with a fly rod. (Huh?) People who are otherwise good fly anglers consistently will have excuses why they didn't catch their big one on a fly. "It was too windy." "The fish were too far out." "It seemed too hard." "Excuse number four." If you want to catch a cobia no matter what, put out a piece of meat on a big heavy rod. If you want to catch a cobia on a fly, fish with a fly rod. Simple.

We were running the beach between Beaufort Inlet and Cape Lookout on a glorious May morning. The water was calm, the sun was shining. We were looking for "bait balls," large accumulations of hand-sized menhaden. These bait balls attract game fish of all species and sizes. Everywhere you look you'll see sharks, bluefish, and Spanish mackerel. But cobia may be elusive if sharks are

Get your fly and your leader rigged and ready for catching cobia.

thick. If you find an eighteen wheeler–sized bait ball with no sharks on it, you have probably found the cobia.

My buddy Scott was driving his beautiful Blackjack center console when we saw what we wanted. We had previously been on some bait balls that were absolutely infested with sandbar and blacktip sharks. This bait ball had no sharks. Right away we saw the cobia swimming around the edge of it. I got my 10-weight with the big baitfish fly tied on a size 3/0 hook. When I dropped the fly in front of the 50-pounder that was at the lead of the pack, a smaller one came out from behind and slurped it in before the big one could move. Now the fight: a screaming run punctuated by tremendous head shakes. The 10-weight may have been a little light; I wished I had used a 12-weight instead. The 20-pound class tippet with a 60-pound shock leader held together. The rod didn't break because I kept the tip low, just about in the water the whole time. ("High sticking" creates forces that break fly rods pretty quickly). Most people gaff cobia, which understandably makes the fish absolutely go berserk. Since

Cobia have huge mouths that enable them to eat anything they want, and powerful tails that they use to good advantage when hooked.

we opted to release this one, I grabbed its tail and cradled its belly with my other hand. This hold will generally calm a large fish, and it works on cobia too. We took a couple quick pictures and let him go. Cobia are a fly rod fish, you just have to use it.

Rod, Flies, and Presentation

A 10-weight rod will work on almost any cobia you are likely to hook, but there are fish over 50 pounds brought into the scales every day. A friend of mine caught a 75-pounder on a heavy spinning rod that took almost an hour to land. A 12-weight would be a better choice in that situation for sure.

A thick-bodied baitfish fly to mimic the menhaden will get bitten. I've used a variety of wiggly patterns, but the fly must have lots of movement without having to strip it out of the strike zone. By the way, that strike zone is right in their faces. You need to cast the fly right on the fish's nose. Get it in there, then strip hard so it jumps. Make long, hard pulls with a pause in between. You may get a follow. If the fly is almost to the boat and the fish appears noncommittal, let it fall below its face and then strip it quickly so it comes up again. This may trigger a strike.

Another trick is to look for swirls in the middle of the bait ball. If the bait starts to swirl out and you see what looks like a whirlpool in the middle, a fish is in there, feeding. Cast in the middle of the swirl with a sinking line; let it sink for a few seconds until it falls below where you can see it. You may be rewarded with a jarring strike or you may get a follow, then you can tease the cobia into striking.

Enticing a Cobia

We had the boat parked over a giant menhaden bait ball. Bluefish and Spanish mackerel were crushing small minnows on the outskirts.

Cobia will shadow huge schools of menhaden all along their range.

I had seen several sharks earlier. A group of cobia had just cruised by out of range and swam under the menhaden school. Right away I saw a big swirl in the middle. It looked like a whirling vortex of fish. I cast my big streamer into the midst and counted down ten seconds before starting my retrieve. A shadow rose out of the gloom to follow my fly. The cobia had its nose right on the fly. It followed right up to my feet. It was now or never as I thought of how muskie anglers tempt following muskies, by moving the rod tip around in a figure-8 next to the boat as a big fish follows.

I started twitching my rod to the side before sweeping my rod in that pattern when the cobia accelerated, engulfing the fly. Usually, I prefer a strip set to drive the hook home, but my rod tip was straight out to the side so I had nowhere to go. I got the hook set as well as I could as the cobia ripped line off my reel. I didn't feel good about an outcome that would be in my favor. It came to a quick conclusion as soon as the fish stopped running and started to shake its significant head. I felt a few thumps followed by the depressing feeling of my line going slack. The hook pulled. Next time, Mr. Cobe.

Finally, keep in mind that cobia like to follow large objects. Sometimes you can find them circling navigation buoys. It is always worth a check when you are near a chain of them, or if there is a single large buoy marking a reef or a wreck. They will also trail along behind leatherback turtles. If you have not seen these turtles, they look like large, black Volkswagen Beetles in the water. Cobia will

Catch a cobia and you will smile like this too.

swim underneath and alongside them. A decent cast will often be rewarded and most times there will be more than one fish. Some anglers look for them exclusively. I've only come across it a couple of times and the cobia were there each time. The leatherbacks really are immense and quite a wonder to see.

During cobia runs along the entire Gulf and Southern Atlantic coastlines, you will see an influx of boats with towers on top as anglers make a mad attempt to catch a fish. The towers are great for added visibility, but you don't absolutely need one. The fish are pretty visible even without riding atop the towers. Anglers get too tempted to make ridiculously long casts with big jigs and never even take a chance with a fly rod. When a cobia swims by, there's a pretty good chance you'll spot it. Then it's a matter of having your rod rigged and ready to go. Make sure it's a fly rod and don't make any excuses.

Chapter Eleven

False Albacore

The fish that gets people fired up.

The fish that still brings the most anglers to North Carolina from all over the world every year are the false albacore that show up around Cape Lookout every fall. Their strength and tenacity on the end of a line combined with the visual nature of chasing them in the shallow water where they are often found makes it a world-class fishery. For a true world-class fly-fishing destination, there has to be a large number of fish in clear, shallow water that can be pursued near the surface on a daily basis, rather than blind casting for hours. Cape Lookout's albies provide all that on most days from mid-October until the end of November. Sometimes it starts earlier and sometimes it goes later, but if you can get out there between Columbus Day and Thanksgiving when the wind is blowing up to 10 knots from the north, I am pretty sure that you will see surface-feeding albies in shallow water. It's what puts Cape Lookout albies up there with southern Louisiana redfish, Islamorada tarpon, and Montauk striped bass.

This is what you come for: albies busting minnows provide a pretty clear indication of where they are.

Finding Fish Is the Tough Part

It was a perfect early November day with a light north wind; jacket temperature, but no need for cold weather gear. I was fishing with my buddy Pete. We were running the beach looking for busting fish.

The schools were small and moving fast. We were having trouble getting into them. I knew that the visible numbers of feeders would increase as it got lighter. Sure enough, I soon saw birds flocking together in 15 feet of water just off the beach. It was as if somebody threw a blanket over the surface and the entire blanket was made of fish. False albacore and minnows covered everything.

Everybody is happy when the albies are biting, and so is Pete Paschall.

Pete made a great cast with a small glass minnow imitation on a size-2 hook, immediately hooking up to his first albie of the season. The first run is the reason for chasing false albacore because they are downright inedible. Some guys who are more full of machismo than anything else like to brag how they stop that first run. That's stupid to try because you can break off the fish and bruise your knuckles, maybe both. The whole thing is the first run. They zip at 40 miles per hour like a bonefish on steroids. The reel makes that great sound as the line cuts through the water.

The hardest part about this fishing can be simply finding the fish. Be prepared to run 20 or 30 miles a day sometimes. Not offshore, nope. Along the shore, side to side, as it were. Having a network of guys with cell phones is helpful. A quick text message exchange between friends is a great way to cover the search area.

The Dos and Don'ts

When the fish are shallow, be careful how you approach them. Coming in too hot can put them off, although sometimes you have to drive the boat more aggressively to get into them. Each day is different. I will say the early-season fish that are a little smaller tend to be more easily put down by boat noise than the bigger fish that arrive later in the season. Be prepared for anything when the bigger fish make their appearance.

The first run took all of Eamon Lee's fly line and a nice chunk of his backing.

An albie over 18 pounds will take you on a ride. When you hook one you'll know. All your gear had better be in prime condition. Your knots had better be good, because you can lose your fly line if they're sloppy. Your fish-fighting technique better be right, or you will break your rod. Your reel had better be smooth, or it will fall apart. Keep the tip low and almost in the water when the fish is under the boat near the end of the battle. If you lift your rod tip above 90 degrees, it's only a matter of time before physics comes into play and snaps that tip off.

The bigger fish eat a wider variety of baits too. Usually it's enough to be prepared with size-2 glass minnow imitations, but some bigger flies will be helpful at times too. I've seen them feeding on hand-sized herring, ballyhoo, and menhaden. You name it, they'll eat it. But day-in and day-out, a slim fly about the size and shape of a grown

This is the reward.

man's middle finger will entice most albies. A floating line works most of the time. An intermediate line is nice when it gets a little breezy. They are thinner, weigh more, and cut the wind easier. Sometimes the fish will be in deep water around trawlers or you might see them on the depth finder. That is when a sinking line is certainly handy. It's not the most fun way to fish, but sometimes it's all that works.

Pulling up behind a trawler. Check the depth finder for marks. Stay in the wake to stay out of the nets.

True Stories

The two guys fishing with me had nail knots tied into their fly line at 40 feet. Somebody at a fly shop somewhere had told them that was as far as they needed to be able to cast so that was as far as they were going to cast. Period. I shook my head, racking my brain as to how I was going to get these guys a fish. Shrimp trawlers. There was one on the horizon. I cruised up to it and slid into its wake as the guys pulled 40 feet of line off their reels. No more. Ever. The boat was still coasting forward. They each had their flies in the water as they prepared to cast.

Suddenly both of their lines went tight before they had even started. The sinking fly lines had taken the flies down about 10 feet as they got ready to cast and the fish just smoked them. The albies went straight down as they are wont to do in such a situation and both guys lifted their rods straight up in the air. Just as I was saying to not do that, their rods snapped in unison. It was like being at a gun range as both wands of expensive graphite went *pop* in quick succession. They were able to hand line their fish to the boat and after a long physics lesson, I reluctantly let them use my rods.

WHEN A CREASE FLY WORKS

Top-water fishing for albies along the beach can be addicting.

To me, the best way to catch them is on top. A popper such as a crease fly is a blast to use, and sometimes the best way to get a bite. There are two times for this. First, it helps if it's not too windy. The popper seems to get lost when it's choppy. If it's a calm day, it's game

"Cast it now! Right there!"

on! If the fish are busting thick, cast your crease fly into the melee and pop it slowly. Give it hard pulls, but not too fast. When they hit, it will be on the pause between strips.

The other good time is the opposite situation. When the fish are running super shallow, in less than 5 feet of water, you can see them swimming past like torpedoes. The problem is you can't get it in front of them quickly enough. That's when a crease fly gets their attention. I've seen them change direction from 30 feet away to come back and smack a popper after they heard its clarion call. In that shallow water there is only one way for a hooked fish to go: away from you toward the ocean. This is when you had better have enough backing on your reel or you might lose the whole taco in ten seconds.

I had two guys from Virginia in the boat with me. It had been a tough day searching for albies. The fish were scattered, while the word on the radio and cell phone was not good. We had been all over. A shot here and a shot there was all we could muster. No hook-ups, but it happens. Nobody said it was going to be easy. We hadn't given up yet and were cruising the beach when it occurred, a huge blow up just out of range.

I got us over just as things were calming down. My angler had a crease fly tied on that I had gotten as a gift from another guy who had gotten it as a gift from a different fisherman. That guy had caught a fish on it and passed it to the other guy who got a fish on it and so on. Karma, right? He made a nice cast into the last receding boil. *Pop. Pop. Bloosh!* That is pretty much the exact sound it makes when a false albacore takes a popper. The guy later remarked that he had never seen so much backing disappear from his fly reel so quickly. He didn't think it was possible for a fish to actually swim that fast. Especially one under 20 pounds on a 10-weight rod.

Griffin Sherron with the high-quality photo bomb.

We ended up casting to the back end of busting schools for the next two hours, hooking up pretty consistently on that Karmic crease fly. It's a pretty exciting style of fishing: world class all the way.

Tuna cruising in the shallows. Well, not tuna exactly, but as close as you're going to see in 15 feet of water around here anyway.

Neill Pollock knows that sometimes your fly has to stand out to be seen.

Further south, false albacore are known as "bonita." Anglers in South Carolina, Georgia, and Florida will pursue them as targets of opportunity whenever they present themselves. Some enterprising anglers have determined that there are drop-offs and reefs where albies are present and will chum with either live or dead bait. It brings the fish up. In this situation, almost any fly will work. This will get you dozens of hook-ups in a pretty short time along with plenty of chances to break some rods. They dare you to pull them up from straight under the boat. Rod tips often go straight back down so be careful.

Chapter Twelve

Amberjack

The amberjack is a worthy adversary on any tackle but really comes into its own when caught on a fly.

Reef donkeys. That's what bottom-fishing dudes looking for grouper and snapper call them. To them, the amberjack is a nuisance, something that gets in the way when they are trying to fill coolers. They pull really hard and are exceedingly aggressive. They bust tackle and backs. To me, those are all indicative of a fish I'd really like to catch on a fly. It just so happens they are really awesome and do the exact things that we as fly anglers love the most: hit on top in clear water!

The B.A. Popper makes a noise that calls them up from deep.

Captain Tom Roller of Waterdog Charters in Beaufort, North Carolina, developed the unique top-water fly-rod tactics we use. Tom said, "They might be the hardest fighting fish, pound for pound, and you can catch them on top-water poppers. What's not to love? North Carolina may have the best 'AJ' fishing in the world, but if you're not careful all your gear will be broken and your back will hurt."

Where to Find Them

If you find a wreck in the 60 (or so) feet of water range with the water temperature above 70°F, chances are that amberjack will be hanging out there. A lot of the wreck locations are listed on the

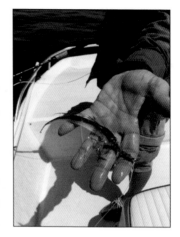

Unfortunately, nothing in life, especially a fly used for amberjack, is permanent.

fishing charts you can buy at local tackle shops. You need a decent GPS unit on your boat; the mapping feature is a nice bonus. Get on your numbers then look for the structure when you get over the wreck. The fish will show as big hooks on the chart. Then it's a simple matter to get a bite. Or is it?

It would seem so, since they are very aggressive and appear ubiquitous when you'd rather catch a grouper. Then, when you actually want to catch one, they get all fussy. Here are a couple of tricks. Cast a jig out on a heavy spinning rod; they will follow the jig back to the boat without hitting it. Same thing if you throw a big streamer on a sinking line (you might catch a cobia, though). For some reason, however, at times these fish will go after a popper like kids running for the house that's giving out full-sized chocolate bars on Halloween. There are days when they won't hit anything; you can see them on the scope, and they come up to the top, but they won't hit.

Happens. Most likely somebody was there bait fishing for them the day before and they were put off.

Terrifying Top-Water Technique

Find a wreck that nobody has been on for a couple days and you're in. Use a 12-weight rod with a floating line. Get a popper with a 1-inch diameter body, a hollowed-out face and a lot of flashy stuff in the tail. Cast it out over the wreck. Pull that line as hard as you can to make as much noise as possible. At first you will see silvery shimmers down deep. Then the whole fish will appear, followed by many more in a hungry pack. Don't stop moving that fly. They will swipe at it and miss it, which makes you whoop and holler. You may not hook up, which is odd to me because their mouths are huge, but keep casting. Eventually, one will connect and now you are in trouble. Because one that is merely in the 30-pound range will take you a good twenty or thirty minutes to haul in, even with a 30-pound leader and 60-pound shock tippet. You just can't horse them in, they are simply too tough and determined, hence the nickname "donkey."

That hole in the water used to be a popper.

This is a common characteristic of all fish in the jacks species. They just won't quit until they are utterly exhausted. If you land them by hand, take a good look around the boat for a second before reaching in the water. Chances are there aren't any big sharks around, but there might be. Even if there are, you probably won't see them, but it makes me feel better anyway. So before I put my arm in the water to grab a fish that's been fighting for thirty minutes over an offshore reef, I take a good long look around. You see what I mean?

My Aching Back

Off every inlet on the North Carolina coast, there are many shipwrecks. It's the "Graveyard of the Atlantic" after all. Rip Woodin and I were going to hit one to get him into an amberjack on a fly. It was blowing a bit stiff from the southwest, but it was supposed to calm down during the day. We noticed it start to change, then the water got glassy. This was looking good. We hit a wreck that was a bit off the beaten path, not that far away but just far enough that it didn't get that much pressure.

We got on the numbers and sure enough the depth-finder screen was full of marks. Rip got up on the bow and started working his line out. It took one cast to determine that the AJs were in a playful mood as they ran up under the foot-long foam popper I had made. It took two casts for one to inhale it and head for wherever it is that big fish head for when we hook them. I settled back to watch the show and offer helpful words of advice. Things like, "How you doing there, Old Man?" and "Your back sore yet?" You know, helpful stuff. You can't rush these fish, but as long as everything holds together, they tend to stay hooked. After a good twenty minutes, some sore arms, and a lot of cranking, we got the fish boatside for the release. Rip said, "That was fun but that may be enough for me."

Then it was my turn. After getting repositioned back over the wreck, I made a long cast. I started my hard popping retrieve. A silvery flash caught my notice to the right. I looked over just in time to see an amberjack just under the surface and swimming fast. Right toward my popper. The fly was consumed in a spray of water reminiscent of Old Faithful. This fish had come from 20 feet below the surface and over 90 feet horizontally to attack this popping and gurgling thing. It just had to be eaten!

They are handsome fish. "Reef Donkey," indeed.

Once again the initial hookup was followed by twenty minutes of the hard-pulling amberjack fight. This time it was my turn to receive helpful advice from Rip. "You look okay up there for an older fella," and "Don't fall in, I bet there are sharks." Again, helpful stuff.

We ended up getting a couple more each before we decided to call it a day. Amberjacks are a great game fish. Not donkeys to be vilified, but a fish worthy of pursuit in its own regard.

These fish will put your skills as an angler to the test—obviously this angler has the skills.

Chapter Thirteen

Mahi Mahi (Dolphin)

This mahi mahi hit a cast fly after being enticed to the boat with a trolled bait.

The fish that normally resides farthest offshore that you can reliably pursue with a fly rod here is the mahi mahi, or dolphin. They swim in the Gulf Stream about 40 miles off Morehead City, farther out near Wilmington, but much closer opposite Hatteras. If you can find the pure, clean water and floating sargassum mats, you will find dolphin. It's a tricky deal to get them close enough so you can cast flies at them, but then it's game on. It's a multiple-rod, team effort that has to be coordinated ahead of time.

You start out (as Russell Chatham said in *The Angler's Coast*) trooooollinggggggg. Ugh. I know, right? But let me finish, there's a trick to it. Get some moderate-sized trolling gear. It doesn't have to be marlin or bluefin tuna rigs, but if you go too light, it's a sure bet you'll hook a wahoo or something bigger that is too much for your tackle. Most of the mahi we find around here are less than 20 pounds with the occasional shot at a bruiser above 30 or 40. So match your tackle to that bigger-sized fish, just in case.

The Technique

Troll with a rigged ballyhoo or some other trolling bait that you can find a picture of on the Internet. It doesn't matter because once you find the fish they'll probably hit it. Check with some friends who fish offshore or subscribe to an online water temperature service to see where the warm water is offshore. It's usually about 20 or so miles out of Morehead City, near or past the 90-foot drop. It's closer if you're a little north, further as you go south through Georgia. Put a bunch of gas in the tank of a big center-console boat. Drive on out there. Slow down when you get to blue water. Got it so far? Now comes the fun part.

Start a troll at 4 to 5 knots. That's fast enough to cover some water but not so fast that your baits fall apart. Fish around where there is sargassum weed on the surface, but not so much that it fouls your gear all the time. Put out as many rods as you think you can handle. But remember, we are not trolling for meat here but to bring the fish to the boat. Have a 10-weight fly rod rigged with a floating line, an 8-foot leader with a 20-pound tippet, and a 3- to 4-inch baitfish fly that includes some blue, silver, and pink, or yellow and green. Get a big, plastic bucket or tub of some kind at the dollar place or even a fancy fly-line bucket from one of the guys who are making them now.

Strip the amount of line that you will be able to quickly pick up and cast, then coil that line carefully inside the bucket. When you get a strike on the trolling lines, and on the good days it doesn't take as long as you might think, reel in the other lines and stop the boat. Someone needs to bring the hooked fish in. I know, tough job, right? In the meantime, another person needs to be ready with the fly rod and to be on the lookout for following fish. Most times they will show under the hooked fish or sometimes right alongside it. If you see one fish right next to the first, cast right beside the hooked fish. The follower will do some kind of gymnastics to get that fly. If there is a school of fish underneath, you will see them flashing.

HAVE SEVERAL RODS READY

Regardless of what you see or do not see (and I cannot stress this enough), do not bring that first fish into the boat until you are absolutely sure there are no others. Leave the trolling rod in the rod holder. Now the second guy can get his rod out. It helps to have several rods ready to go. If you can see the followers and they look to be less than 10 pounds (and they usually are), get out your 8-weight, or even a 6-weight if you feel like living on the edge. Here's the thing, you can be happily casting to a 4-pound mahi in this situation when something much bigger comes from who-knows-where to blast your fly and take off like a rocket. So, maybe stick with the 8-weight. Wahoo and marlin can show up and then you'll have your hands full. Let me know if you catch a wahoo on a fly around here. I want to see the pictures.

After a while, even if the dolphin are still hanging around, they may stop attacking your flies. Try a smaller fly, something in the 2-inch range, maybe all yellow or white. This should entice one or two more. Inevitably, there will come a time when none will be

Captain Tom Roller knows about catching mahi mahi and is a pleasure to have around your kids.

interested; they've seen it all. Take a look at how many fish you have. They are good to eat, they spawn well, and grow fast. Keep a few, it's okay, but let's not get crazy. If you have ten, fifteen or even twenty fish in the box, you've had a great time. It can happen quickly. That's plenty for the neighborhood.

Just Perfect

We were trolling rigged ballyhoo along a weed line in about 95 feet of water. It was June and we were about 20 miles out of Morehead City. The water was beautiful. We were seeing flying fish and turtles everywhere. A bottle-nosed dolphin followed us on the way out. Great. Things got perfect after only five minutes of trolling when

Mahi mahi hit flies well, and they jump and fight like crazy.

one of the rods bent over double and the reel started screaming. A gorgeous mahi mahi came flying out of the water. It was doing cartwheels and twists that would make Simone Biles jealous. My friend Dr. Bogus was on rod duty while I got my fly rod ready.

As he brought the fish in close after its initial display, I noticed right away that there was another fish perfectly mirroring the movements of the hooked fish. When it got within 60 feet of the boat, it was moving directly across the stern going from starboard to port. I dropped a cast directly in front of the hooked fish and to the right of the free swimmer. At this point, the free-swimming fish did a complete twist in the water to get my fly. As I set the hook I said, "Did you see that move?" It was immediately followed by a close-in explosion of water as my now fly-hooked fish started to freak out less than 60 feet off the stern. It jumped like mad and made a beautiful run of about 100 yards. The colors of these fish are amazing. After a couple more jumps, I was able to get the fish boatside. There was nobody to help me land my fish because the other two guys with me were too busy fighting their fish. We enjoyed a solid hour of casting to and hooking up with mahi mahi in the 10- to 12-pound range.

Get on out to the Gulf Stream with a fly rod. The water is beautiful and the golden mahi mahi are a great reward worthy of any quest. It's why they call them "El Dorado" in Mexico.

Chapter Fourteen

"Other" Fish

Catching croakers is a fun pastime.

S ometimes you just need to have an open mind. Running down the beach on fall mornings around Cape Lookout, means you are looking for false albacore. Pete and I both saw the shower of baitfish at the same time. "What was that?"

Jack Crevalle

"I don't know but let's get over there." I hopped up on the bow with 10-weight in hand and a crease fly tied on. We both looked one way and saw giant fish rushing through the water, so big that I initially thought they were dolphins. Then I looked the other way and all hell broke loose in front of me as giant jack crevalle were tearing it up. I laid my popper in there and hardly moved it before it was engulfed by a cavernous mouth. In what seemed like microseconds, it ripped all my line and most of my backing from my reel. Things were going south rapidly when I noticed Pete limbering his rod.

"Hey buddy, I want you to have a shot at these too but I think I am about to get spooled." So he fired up the motor and we gave chase. I finally got the fly line back on the reel when it all got pulled out again. At this point I was seriously concerned about my backing knot and really hoped I had it tied perfectly because I was sure my fly line was going to get broken off. After several more knuckle-busting runs and over an hour later, we had the fish boatside. The fight was still not over.

We were sitting in 40 feet of water by this time. Every time we'd get the fish up, it would go back down. Finally, it rolled over on its side. It was a massive slab of silver. Pete reached down and got his hands around the tail but couldn't lift it up over the gunwale. It took both of us to wrestle the fish out of the water and into the boat. When I draped it across my lap for a photo, it left a blanket of slime on my legs that I wore with pride. We released that hardened battler and it swam off like nothing had happened. Checking out length/girth to weight ratio charts made me pretty sure it was well over 50 pounds. That's still my biggest catch on a fly in North Carolina. It wasn't the fish we were looking for, and in fact the albies didn't do much the rest of the day, but I was glad to have gotten the chance at a spectacular game fish.

Be prepared to spend some time when you hook into a jack crevalle like this.

Tripletail

Tripletail sometimes migrate through Georgia and Florida waters. In the "Golden Isles" of Georgia, they present a unique sight-fishing opportunity. According to Captain David Edens, you can simply idle around looking for floating fish. They look like trash bags in the water.

"When you spot one, put the trolling motor down and get close enough to cast a lightly weighted shrimp or baitfish imitation," Edens

advised. "They may or may not eat it." Apparently they are pretty persnickety. I've never caught one so that's one more to add to the list.

Captain David Edens shows off a tripletail. That wide tail and thick head add up to a tough, spirited fighter.

Tarpon

While it's pretty much common knowledge that tarpon migrate well up the coast into the Chesapeake Bay, bait anglers catch most of them. They set up and do the "bait and wait" game. Fly anglers have caught a couple in North Carolina waters over the years. Anglers in South Carolina and Georgia target them on a fly as well. Again, this is not something you can say is going to happen every day. It's a limited location and a small time window that of course is made smaller due to the vagaries of wind and weather.

Fishing with Kids

Ladyfish like this fight more like tarpon than anything but a tarpon itself.

I have caught sixty-nine different species of fish on a fly rod. Not all of them have them have been what you'd called glamorous. To go along with the redfish, bonefish, and striped bass, there are also ladyfish, croaker, puffer, and toadfish. I've even caught a sea robin on a top-water fly! One great thing to consider is that usually these less prestigious fish cannot only save the day when it's slow, they can make the day when you are accompanied by a youngster.

Find a tidal outflow in a marsh. Hit it on the outgoing tide. Give the kid a push-button reel with a small jig on the line. Put a piece of shrimp or something on the hook. Show him (or her) how to cast. They'll throw it out there and chances are there will be croakers, baby sea bass, spots, toadfish, and who knows what else. Watch for smiles. Bonus if there is a hard sand bottom. Perfect for getting out and exploring when the tide gets really low. Kids love splashing around on low tide flats. Love is what this is about, after all.

Kid + Croaker + Mud = Fun

Chapter Fifteen

Flies

Wake up on a calm morning. No wind, hardly any clouds: A perfect day for fishing. There's been no rain in a while so the water is going to be clear, and you should be able to do some sight fishing. The reds have been schooled up in a hard-bottomed sandy area where you'll be able to see them. This makes you happy. You hop right in the truck that you hitched and loaded up last night; off you go. Your buddy is waiting at the ramp, the boat launches perfectly, and you are on your way to the spot. A coin flip puts your buddy on the poling tower first. When you get to the spot, the light is just right so you can see some wakes of feeding fish. This should be perfect.

A stocked fly box getting ready to hit the water.

Simply Ignored

You tie on a fly created in a moment of inspiration that you were sure would be perfect. It's got everything on it, including rubber legs. The water is about 8 inches deep. The boat is not making noise by rubbing the bottom. Everything is perfect. Here they come. You make a good 60-foot cast. Leading the school by about 4 feet. The lead fish swims right up to your fly and . . . goes right over it. The next fish does the same. You can see the fish as they tip down and dart to the side—they are obviously feeding. You cast again. Same thing happens; they totally ignore your offering. The school swims off unmolested. Your buddy poles frantically to reposition the boat. You try again. Same result. Finally, after the fifth cast, you get one to eat. You whoop it up and everybody is happy. But what really happened? Let's take it one step at a time.

Flies in various states of readiness either awaiting their coat of adhesive or drying out.

Redfish are the ultimate opportunistic predators that will eat anything if given the chance. Their mouth is situated in the middle of their head and they can feed up or down in the water column with equal aplomb. Having said that, sometimes they get picky. On white sand flats under a clear sky, you have the toughest situation. Let's start with that buggy, rubber-legged fly. In dark water, with weeds and siltation, you normally want a fly that is brightly colored and pushes a lot of water: palmered hackles, big collars, fuzzy rabbit hair bodies and things like that will help a fly get noticed. In clear water the opposite is usually required. Muted colors, slimmer profiles, more realistic silhouettes. There's a reason that thin baitfish

This conehead fly was an experiment that worked but needed refining because it didn't resist snagging as well as I would have liked. Now there are products on the market that do a better job at what I was trying to accomplish here.

patterns catch more fish in more places than anything else. They work!

Another good choice for redfish in clear water is a permit-style crab pattern. The point being that in darker, murkier waters a fly with a brighter color pattern and a bigger profile works due to its increased visibility. Combine that with the fact that often those murky creeks are packed full of juvenile mullet, shrimp, and crabs, and your fly has a lot work to do. In clearer water, a brightly colored fly, or a fly with an unrealistic profile may be ignored or even avoided. So, use more realistic flies in clearer water, and brighter and bushier flies in murky water. Got it? Let's move on.

Prey Varies, Even Hour to Hour

Prey species vary from location to location, flat to flat, day to day and even hour to hour. Sometimes it seems that fish will eat whatever you put in front of them. On other occasions they are maddeningly selective. What does this mean? Having a basic understanding of prey items available in a given area is very useful.

Probably the most prevalent little critter available anywhere in saltwater is a crab of some kind. I have read that crabs (and crustaceans in general) are more prevalent under water than insects are in air. That's pretty astounding when you look at the ground and realize there is always a bug somewhere. Does this mean that crustaceans are always what the fish are eating? Probably not. Does it make for a good place to start when choosing a fly for the day? Definitely. Do you need to have an ultrarealistic crab fly? Some permit guys in Florida are tying amazing-looking stuff now. Those flies are finding their way into fly boxes being used for redfish by anglers in more pressured fisheries like Biscayne Bay and Mosquito Lagoon in Florida, but they are not always needed.

Usually, the presentation beats the pattern. Fish a fly the way you can imagine a certain creature behaving and anything could work. Shrimp swim with a certain jerky pattern; a couple fast jumps and a pause. Crabs can move quite quickly along the bottom, and when they stop, they swing their claws around, even the little ones, like they're tough. Minnows move pretty steadily, except for the ones not having a good day. Injured or sick baitfish will move slowly and often stop swimming. This is a trigger for gamefish.

I once made a presentation at the fish tank at Bass Pro Shops in Concord, North Carolina, about how to fish a Clouser Minnow to imitate all these. I cut the hook point off and wouldn't you know it, a crappie ate the thing. Redfish smacking schooling minnows on a flat will break the surface. A baitfish profile will be just the ticket. If you see a school of fish moving slowly down a shoreline and sporadic breaks on the surface with shrimp jumping clear, a Seaducer will work just fine. If you see redfish moving slowly along over a flat with an occasional flash of gold as one turns one way or the other, then a crab imitation will be just the ticket. These strategies can be applied to any fish that you see feeding anywhere, whether they are in a school or feeding alone.

Which Prey to Copy?

Now we have put some thought into which prey species we need to copy. Of course you want to "invent" a brand new fly to imitate something. Great! Keep in mind before you go naming your "new" fly after yourself, that most innovations in fly tying have already taken place, whether it's a fly pattern or some technique that presents the fly in a different manner. There really isn't a whole lot of "new" out there. It's probably been done before. The real new stuff is in the

If the bait is small, you might need an equally tiny fly to get any interest from the fish feeding on them.

materials that we have available to use along with some tools and adhesives that seem to keep popping up from truly inventive people.

Most of the new flies I see are merely recreations of flies invented years ago. Having said that, there are some cool flies out there utilizing the myriad new materials. There is indeed nothing wrong with using your imagination to imitate something you are seeing and not readily able to find. That is much of the fun of fly tying: seeing it in the wild then making it at your desk.

CONSIDER A SHRIMP

Let's think about a shrimp fly. Shrimp are readily available to fish and it seems that everything out there eats them. A lot of patterns we see are overly complicated to achieve maximum realism. Many times what works best is a fly that creates an impression of the shrimp or other prey item. I believe Monet would have been a great fly tier. In our scenario we are talking about fishing clear flats in a foot or less of water with sandy bottom. In this situation we want a fly that is not too bright, that looks pretty realistic, sinks quickly without being too heavy (which would make them difficult to cast and land noisily), and we probably don't need to worry about weeds. Usage will make this fly very specific.

A fly that works in our situation will need to be totally different from one that works in murky water with muddy bottom and weeds. Another note before we go on, many good flats anglers will tie multiple versions of the same fly with the only difference being the amount of weight contained in the fly: a heavier dumbbell eye for deeper flats, less weight for shallower flats, and an unweighted version for tailing fish in water that isn't much deeper than morning dew.

So let's get back to our new fly; a shrimp has long antennae, buggy eyes, lots of wiggly legs, a segmented body and swimmer fins on its tail. Take a good look at a photo, or even better, hold a live one in your hand. Put it in a bucket and watch how it moves. Put all the pieces together and be prepared to toss your first try in the trash (better yet, cut it all off, save the hook and start over). If you observe and think, you'll come up with something good. My favorite shrimp fly is the Seaducer, which, considering the previous line of thought here, was invented by Chico Fernandez, but then discovered to have been invented by Joe Brooks fifty years previously; great minds see things similarly. If I take a Seaducer and add some weighted eyes of different sizes, and maybe some kind of estaz material to wrap the hackle around, I have a variation that may work better than the standard one in all the books. So sometimes it's not inventing a whole new fly, but just coming up with a variation on a standard pattern to match the situation.

Now we have our new fly. It's two weeks later. There haven't been any significant storms since the last time you went, and a nice weather window comes up with similar tides. Nobody has been bothering those fish that you know about. You and your buddy get out again. This time he gets the bow first and you offer him one of your new flies; he graciously accepts. On the way out to the flat you really hope the fish are still there. You shut down and start poling. Of course, you start from far enough away that you don't spook the fish. You would never run right onto a flat. That's just rude. You'd spook the fish and possibly ruin the flat for yourself and any future anglers. Also it messes up any grass growing there.

After poling for about fifteen minutes, you see what you were looking for. The school shows up as a black blob moving across the bottom. The wind is blowing lightly from left to right and the sun is behind you, a perfect setup. Your buddy is within range and makes a perfect 80-foot cast. The fly lands about 5 feet in front of the lead fish in the school that is moving right toward it. You're getting pumped now.

Redfish in super shallow water push a big wake when they move to feed on shrimp and small minnows.

Suddenly, two fish near the front accelerate rapidly; you see a wake as they rush toward the fly. They are competing over who gets it! The bigger fish gets there first, tips its head down, flares its gills as it opens its mouth, and the fly is gone. Your buddy strips his line to come tight and the fight is on. Your new fly is a success! The redfish makes a nice long run into the backing after the hookup. You pole the boat away from the school to keep from spooking the rest of them. The fish stubbornly comes to the boat after a couple of more runs. Lights, camera, release. Switch places and after it again. It's a beautiful day filled with beautiful fish, made all the more perfect because you figured out the solution to a vexing problem.

Basic Fly Tying

If you are a beginning fly tier, learn how to tie these flies first. They cover all the basic fly-tying techniques. With a tweak in color and/or

The classics of coastal fishing: Lefty's Deceiver, Clouser Deep Minnow, Chico's Seaducer. I firmly believe that a selection of these in different sizes and colors will have an angler prepared to fish anywhere in the world.

size, they will catch fish anywhere in the world. They were developed by some of the greatest names in our sport. I'm not going to list extensive instructions or close-up pictures. Fly-tying instructional videos on YouTube are very helpful and much more useful. I use those videos all the time.

Chico Fernandez created the Seaducer as a tarpon fly. It's a great shrimp imitation and can be tied with or without a weed guard, but I usually add one. Bob Clouser created the Clouser Deep Minnow as a smallmouth bass fly, but it catches everything that swims. Depending on how you fish it, it can imitate a slim minnow on top, a crab or shrimp on bottom, or whatever else you need it to be. Lefty Kreh's Lefty's Deceiver is the original herring or shad imitation. Most new streamers are variations on this original design.

Unique Flies I Use

I was solo poling my skiff from the bow. The flat was pretty much in the backyard of some fancy houses and a family I knew was out watching me and saying hello. I looked to my right and I saw a tail pop up, probably the biggest one I had seen all summer. It was September and the tailing season would be over in a few more weeks. I was able to cast to this fish from my boat that I had positioned behind a fallen tree. This would help to mask my position. The cast seemed good, but the fish had changed direction while the fly was in the air. At this point I had to wait until the fish moved away before I picked up to recast so as not to spook it. I cast again and this time it was right on. The fly was barely visible, and I was able to watch the fish swim over, open its mouth and suck it in. It was beautiful! For some reason I was only using my 6-weight when I usually use an 8-weight. Also I only had 10-pound tippet where I would usually use 15. So I had to be extra-careful with this fish, plus I had to keep it

The Critter tied on a plastic worm hook for weedless fishing and the B.A. Popper for B.A. fish.

away from the branches of the same tree that had masked my position. Oh, the irony was dripping. When I got the fish to hand it was a gorgeous specimen and all was right with the world.

CRITTER FLY

My favorite inshore redfish fly is one that was dubbed the Little Crabby Critter by some guys on an Internet forum a few years back. These days I just call it The Critter. It's a tail made of craft fur, a wrapped body with rubber legs, and a wing of some kind. Again, as you'll notice with my flies, the basic simplicity of the design gives an infinite combination of choices. You'll see tiers who have "invented" this fly all over the place, time and again. It's nothing new, but it works because of the ability to change the colors and materials without getting locked into a specific "pattern." If you're fishing over light sand, you can use a tan color; in clear water over dark bottom, then white works great; in murky water, brighter colors get the nod. The same basic design can work in any of those situations.

I have caught all the typical inshore species on them—reds, flounder, trout, stripers. It's just a way of looking at the inshore environment and being prepared for the situations you will be encountering. Using a plastic worm hook allows this version to be fished weedless in situations that call for it. If the water is a little deeper, I can add some lead wrap to the shank. If it's shallow, I leave it alone. Again, have them prepared ahead and be ready to switch as needed.

B.A. POPPER

The amberjacks were lighting up the screen on the depth finder. We simply could not get a bite. I was fishing a streamer fly on a sinking line. They would follow it up through the water column and turn away at the boat. It was the same thing with jigs on a spinning rod. I decided, kind of on a whim, to try a Big Ass Popper I had sitting in my fly box. My buddy, Captain Tom Roller, told me to try it. I had another rod with a floating line already rigged.

The first time that popper hit the water and started making some noise it was like a dinner bell ringing. Those jacks could not help themselves, and I would get three or four hits per retrieve sometimes. We caught them that way until we were too tired to do it anymore. There's something about the gurgling noise that makes those amberjacks decide now is the time to eat. It's amazing really.

The B.A. Popper is easy to make. You can get the bodies at any fly or craft shop, although they'll be much cheaper at the craft shop. Get the 1-inch diameter hard foam popper bodies. You may have to do some trimming to get them to fit on whatever hook you have. A 4/0 or

The Lazer Minnow tied with Senyo's Laser Dub and a homemade popper that will work for bass, redfish, and speckled trout.

5/0 hook with a long, flashy tail made of Ultra Hair or some other long synthetic material will work. Don't use bucktail. It's too expensive and it's not needed here. It's the noise and the profile these fish can't resist.

LASER MINNOW

The albies were firing on all cylinders, but I just could not put it together. I'd get a bite, fight the fish, and it would come off. I'd make a good cast, and the fish would come up, look at my fly, and not commit. I was snake bitten. I told my friend Chris to get up there before I went kind of crazy. He got one good shot and I saw his fly get devoured instantly. We got that one in and I told him to do it again, so he did. Now I had to know, what's the deal? His fly was almost a dead ringer for the little silversides. The material seemed to hold light differently. I had to have one. I beat Chris up with a bat I carry in the boat for just such purposes and, well, not really. Chris gave me one unbidden because that's the kind of guy he is. I immediately hooked up, so the story had a happy ending with no broken bones.

Senyo's Laser Dubbing is a new material to me. Apparently, it's been around for a while, I just missed it. It makes a really nice bait-fish fly that the albies seem to enjoy. Believe me when I say almost anything will work on these fish. When they are feeding, the most important thing is to get your fly in front of their faces. They'll probably eat it. A big part of it too is having confidence in whatever you have tied on. If you feel good about your fly, you'll probably fish better. It's the same as a golfer with a lucky putter or a concert violinist with his favorite bow. Anything would work, but that special thing just makes it better. The original Laser Dub is only 2 inches long, but now they make a version called Bruiser Blend with longer fibers that will make a bigger fly.

HOMEMADE POPPER

This was a new pond, well, new for me anyway. A friend had told me about it. Cool. I'll give it a shot. On my second cast a 5-pound bass came out of nowhere, jumped once, then ran my leader under a drainage pipe and busted me off, all in about three seconds. Ugh. I spent the next hour and a half having a great time catching fish after fish in the 13- to 18-inch range on my 6-weight rod. The small poppers I had made on size-4 hooks with the craft-fur tails seemed to be a delight for these fish, which delighted me as well.

Summer evenings, fly-rod poppers, and bass ponds were made for each other like Clapton and the blues. Casting a popper into a bass pond while the frogs and crickets conduct their symphonies makes a summer day melt into perfection. I came up with this one day while I was messing around with a piece of foam I had lying around. It's not an earth-shattering innovation, it just shows what you can do when you have various materials around and a problem to solve.

I started cutting it up with a pair of scissors until I had a shape I liked, then poked a hole through it with a fly-tying bodkin. Secure the whole thing onto a predressed hook using some super glue and that's it: simple and effective. I got a 3-pounder on it the very first time I took it out. Get the foam blocks or cylinders that are available at any craft store. I like to whittle them with scissors. They make a nice gurgle sound that the fish like too. Sometimes you might end up with one that doesn't quite work. It's all part of the ongoing experiment.

Chapter Sixteen

Equipment

Enough rods to get through the whole trip.

There are guys out there who will tell you that to catch a fish on a fly, you need a rod that costs $900 or a reel that costs $1,000. That's dumb. There's a ton of good gear being manufactured these days. You should be able to find a quality outfit that costs less than your monthly grocery bill. Do some research. Look around at what's out there. Determine how much time you will spend using it.

If you are primarily going to stalk redfish with occasional jaunts to the blue, then get yourself a good quality 8-weight outfit. The reel for redfish doesn't need to stand up to the blistering runs of a marlin, but maintenance should be easy and able to withstand an occasional dunking or getting some mud on it.

Buy a good quality line. The best ones are over $70 now. Good deals can sometimes be found on the shopping sites or in closeout bins online. Don't get the "Tropical" or "Bonefish" lines unless you are specifically using it only during summer. Those are for water over 75°F. As soon as it gets a little chilly, when some of our best fishing of the year takes place, they will get kinky. Conversely, don't get the "Striped Bass" lines as they are meant to be used in cool water and will shrivel up like an overcooked piece of spaghetti in a southern summer. The regular "Saltwater" or even "Bass" lines will suffice for most of our needs. Basically, get what your budget—and your conscience—can endure, then go have fun with it. There's too much ego associated with some guys who have the fanciest gear. Don't listen to them. Expensive equipment doesn't equate to angling expertise.

Something That Floats

Boats are a requirement for fishing coastal waters; not really much way around it. Oh, you can catch a pond bass or maybe a bluefish around the inlets within driving distance. A ferry ride to Cape Lookout may yield a shot at a false albacore busting close enough to shore to reach with a long cast. There are a few other examples of catching fish on foot, but most of the time you will be wishing you could just get "over there." You have options.

Obviously you can go out and buy a fancy boat and there are some real beauties out there, gorgeous boats that can get you there fast and in style. You can also get a kayak, which is a real popular option for fishing the inshore waters. Whatever you get, it won't do everything. That is just the nature of boats. My 16-foot Ankona Copperhead poling skiff that floats in 5½ inches of water and poles without a sound is not the right boat for going out to the wrecks for amberjack or to the Gulf Stream for mahi.

A well-equipped and maintained boat is a pleasure to use for fishing, as Scott Sherron can attest.

Conversely, good luck getting that 25-foot Contender into my favorite redfish creek—it ain't gonna happen. Find a boat that will suit most of the fishing you want to do, then figure out the rest. I will say that a 21-foot bay boat will probably get you to most of the fish on my list if you pick your days and tides properly.

Other Necessities

I always carry a multi-tool. For fishing, I prefer one with a small scissors on it. I use it to trim knots and cut heavy line all the time. Also, if I can't flick the pliers out one-handed, it's useless. With a well-hooked fish in one hand, I can reach for the tool, flick the pliers out and pop the hook out with the other. A good pair of sunglasses is a necessity. Most of the top brands are good. I prefer the kind you would wear to the coast of the sea. Nonscratch lenses are a required investment. Do you carry your smartphone with you fishing? Is it waterproof? If not, get a waterproof case or you'll regret it.

Fly boxes are becoming quite expensive. I'm still using the plastic ones with the brass hinges and the foam inserts that I got over a decade ago, so use that information any way you wish. Do you have a favorite minor league baseball team? Get one of their hats to wear. I never wear the hat of a tackle manufacturer unless they've given me something first. Free advertising is not my thing but supporting my favorite team just comes naturally. You might want to get one of those spandex face-covering doo dads. I use mine primarily in winter. In summer, I like a spray-on sunscreen to cover all exposed areas

A long brim baseball cap and some quality sunglasses help you see the fish and protect your eyes. A good graphite pushpole gets you there quietly.

of my face. I don't like having my nose and mouth covered up. It's my own weird thing.

There are some really fancy gear bags available too. I used to have one, but it didn't last very long in the marine environment. The zippers get stuck then break when tugged. For the past five years I've been using nylon drawstring bags like my son uses to carry his sneakers to basketball practice. All my fly boxes fit in them along with an extra reel and spools. For leader material, I get the stuff that's on the bigger loop spools. I use mono to build my leaders and fluorocarbon for heavy-bite tippets. There is usually a spool of single-strand wire in there too, but it doesn't get used unless some big bluefish show up.

Three guys with face protection from the wind on a cold morning and one without. Guess who was cold?

I use a wearable stripping basket about 90 percent of the time and I don't understand why more people don't. In the boat it keeps my line from getting tangled or blown overboard. When wading, it keeps the line clear of weeds and shells or tangling underfoot. All it takes is a simple

Snails carry all their gear with them everywhere and it doesn't cost them anything.

line management issue for you to miss a shot at a great fish. If you're prepared in advance, you won't get caught by surprise.

Chapter Seventeen

Improving Your Casting

Game on! Is your casting up to the challenge?

I't's game on! You're up on the bow of your friend's boat in the middle of an epic fall blitz. He invited you to go with him to check it out and here you are in the middle of it. The fish are busting like crazy, flying right out of the water! You can't believe it. It's just like the magazine articles and television shows. The fish are up against the beach and the wind is coming strong into your face. You can't get on the upwind side because it's too shallow. They are about 80 feet away. You cast. Your line piles up short. You strip in and cast again. It comes up short again.

Your buddy sees this, "Let's see if we can get you a shot from the upwind side." When he finally gets the boat about 60 feet away—right in your range—the fish go down. "They'll come back up again." And again they do, rampaging on baitfish. Once again you get to your casting range and the fish go down. The fish are a little nervous about the boat in the shallow water and no matter what you do they will not continue feeding once the boat gets closer than 60 or 70 feet. It's frustrating to say the least and you go home with stories of what might have been vowing to do better next time.

This event repeats itself many times throughout the season. People are fired up about getting into a big fish but haven't done their homework so they don't hook up. Can you hook a big fish at 50, 40, 30 feet or less? Yes, of course you can; it happens often. I've actually hooked them under my feet as I was standing on the bow. I've also hooked them at the end of a cast where all my fly line was out of my reel to the backing knot. If I hadn't been able to cast that far, I would not have caught those fish.

Practice in All Conditions

You don't have to be a champion caster who goes to practice ponds and competes in long-distance casting contests to catch fish, but you need to practice more than you probably do. The good saltwater fly angler can reasonably be expected to make a 70- to 80-foot cast with two or three false casts into a mild breeze on the bow of a moderately moving boat. Now the problems occur when the conditions change.

Can you still make that cast when the wind is in your face? How about when it's whipping at your back? With a strong breeze at your back, the wind will carry out your line but it messes up your back cast, and if you're not using a basket, it will throw loose line around your feet. How about when it's a little bit choppy? I don't love standing up there when the waves are crashing over the bow, but a bit of a chop often makes it easier to approach fish. You need to be able to get up there, balance yourself, manage your line, and still make that cast. You should keep false casting to a minimum. It's very frustrating to watch somebody make four or five (or more) false casts while the fish are feeding in front of him. You need to be able to shoot it out there with three or fewer false casts.

Now you're probably saying, "Well that's great and all, but what do I do about it?" If you ask, then I will tell. Get out and practice. Find a pond, a pool, a big lawn, or a softball field. Something. There are a few things you can do to improve when you get there. Keep your wrist

I was casting to a large, laid-up redfish in Louisiana. My guide, Greg, told me to cast closer. I laid it within 12 inches and the fish inhaled it.

firm. If your line is hitting the ground behind you, it's because your wrist is breaking on your back cast. Learn to double haul. A haul is a sharp tug on the line with your line hand while your rod hand moves the rod through an arc and . . . oh, man. You know what? Forget it. Buy any Lefty Kreh fly-casting book. Seriously, read anything he's written about casting. Watch any video he ever made about casting. Go to a demonstration at one of the winter fly-fishing shows where he is appearing. If he is doing casting lessons, take one. Pay if you have to. I mean it. The guy has a real gift for breaking it down for people.

I thought I was a real hot shot when I was younger, and I could probably cast as well as, if not better than, most people. He watched me cast for ten seconds at a show in Charleston then made one off-hand comment that told me how much more I had to learn. Those days are gone now. I don't get to fish as much as I used to, so my casting arm gets sore a little sooner, but I still find the time to practice. Do it. Now! Go!

Practice on a local farm pond, golf course pond, or just a lawn. But practice a lot.

Chapter Eighteen

Saltwater Fly Fishing with Guides

This angler was awaiting instruction from his guide. I hope it was good.

This is the kind of thing I hear from people all the time, "We went saltwater fly fishing with Captain Bubba, who told us that the same redfish he's been catching on shrimp would be perfect on a fly. I guess it was a slow day or something because he had us casting Clousers to the bank all day while he ran his trolling motor. All we caught was a flounder and a little trout."

It wasn't a slow day. Captain Bubba doesn't know anything about fly fishing. There is so much wrong with that statement that I am going to break it down piece by piece. Captain Bubba is a bait fisherman. You can fish with bait and catch fish that would not chase a fly because a neutral or negative-attitude fish is still not going to resist a live shrimp hanging in his face. For fly fishing, you have to find the fish that are in active feeding locations. That means out of main channels and deep holes onto flats where the fish are going to be moving and feeding. The Clouser Minnow is a great fly that has probably caught millions of fish over the years, but it's not always the best choice. Your really good fly guides are going to have their own flies that they have developed from their observations during their time on the water.

Good Guide Traits

Most good guides don't use a Clouser very much, not because it won't work—it definitely will—but because they have developed something else that they are very proud of. The Clouser and other famous patterns are good overall flies, but the specific fly for the specific place that is tied by a thoughtful, observant guide should work better. If the guide you are going with doesn't have his own pattern, or even worse, tells you to bring your own, he doesn't know. Catching redfish on a fly means you have to be in water that is too shallow for a trolling motor. It means push poling. You must go to a specific spot where the guide knows the fish will be on a shallow flat and feeding in a specific manner. Then you must cast to specific fish that you can see. This applies to catching most species of fish on a fly.

If you are casting flies in water that is too deep to see the bottom while using a trolling motor, then the guide is a "Fly Fishing Poser," and you won't catch anything meaningful unless you see feeding fish busting on top. The very fact that the angler in the above scenario caught a small trout means they were fishing in water that wasn't going to be holding anything decent. Unless they were actually fishing for speckled trout, it was more of a search effort than casting to a specific spot, because the guide knew Mr. Red lived there.

If you want to fish shallow water with a fly rod properly, you have to use a push pole.

This fish was in a specific spot that I knew about. I tied a fly to suspend or sink slowly in colors I knew would appeal to them from past experience, which allowed this angler to catch a gorgeous 5-pounder.

The best saltwater fly-fishing guides are unusual. They would rather catch a fish on a fly than any other way. If your guide talks about how he fishes with bait or casting gear when he fishes by himself, or if all the photos you see of him are using spinning rods, move on. The really good saltwater fly-fishing guides are observant, creative, good fly tiers, and have their own unique flies for the fishing they do. They are great fly anglers themselves and know how to work out problems. If you find a guide like this, fish with him every chance you get. You will learn more about fishing and catching fish on a fly than you will learn by yourself in a year. These things will serve you well no matter where you fish in the world.

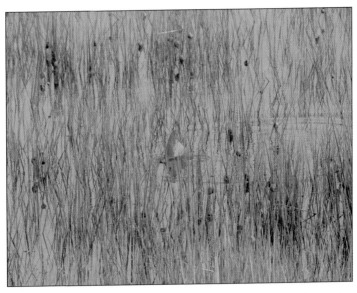

A good fly-fishing guide will know where this happens in his neighborhood, will have developed his own fly, and will have the proper equipment to get to it.

Guides Teach Other Guides

My batting average on bonefish was a perfect .000. I had been to the Keys a bunch of times but never caught one, though I had seen many while fishing on foot. I was even in the Bahamas many years ago. The wind blew so hard for three days we could barely get the boats out, let alone do any meaningful fishing. Now I was in Oahu with my wife for a week. I was going to try bonefishing again. I had heard about this guide there named Captain Jesse Cheape. I gave him a call and reserved a day in the middle of the week.

I asked him, "Are there any places I could drive to and give it a try on my own?" He gave me very specific instructions on a place to go, the tide to fish and a fly to try. But even though that is good information, it doesn't cover everything. I went to the spot and the

An Oahu bonefish flat.

fish were right where Jesse said they would be. I spooked every last one of them into the middle of the Pacific.

The next day I met up with Jesse. I told him about my experience the day before and he nodded, explaining my problem. Bonefish are not redfish. You don't cast as close to them as you do redfish and you fish the fly differently. The fly has to be right on the bottom and you lead them further than you think necessary. Once I got that straight, I caught some nice bonefish and had a great day. I went out again the next morning to the drive-up spot and the fish were there again, but this time, with the knowledge I gained from Jesse, and one of his flies, I caught one that ran out all my fly line, twice. Catching fish with the guide was great, but getting one on my own after learning the missing pieces of my puzzle? Amazing! Thanks, Jesse.

Thanks to his expertise, knowledge, and teaching ability, Jesse was able to get me into some great bonefish action.

Now let me add that just because a guide is not a fly guide doesn't mean he is a bad guide. If you want to cast plugs and spinnerbaits or soak bait for giant bull redfish, I know just the guys who will create a fun and successful outing. If you want to catch fish with a fly, I have a list of guides around the country who are really superb. It's a short list because, as you can see, I have pretty high expectations. Ask me, I'll tell you.

Knowledgeable guides develop their own fly patterns based on personal observation and experience.

Chapter Nineteen

Fishing the Shallows

Getting shallow means going in where others may not be able to get.

The tide charts told me that it would be a good day to find low-tide tailers on a favorite widgeon grass flat. This spot is normally under 3 to 4 feet of water; most people don't know it's there. With my small poling skiff, I go in on low tide when most folks fish around the high water. I skipped along the edge of the shallowest areas to get back into my spot. The widgeon grass was barely, but perfectly exposed. With my eyes scanning for signs of fish, I saw a slight swirl. This was followed by a tail flopping above the surface. I snapped my push pole into the clip I was wearing on my belt, got my rod out of the basket in which it was stashed around my waist, and made my shot.

For once I made a perfect cast the first time. The fish saw my size-2 shrimp pattern, rushed in, and ate. Awesome! After getting that one in, I continued off the edge of that flat into a slightly deeper spot. The water went from 6 inches to 10. There was a big stingray mudding along. It was making a big mess while flapping its wings and . . . wait . . . there was a fish swimming along behind the ray! When I cast in front of and to the side of the ray, the redfish darted out to snap it up. By picking my tide with cooperative sunlight, I was able to have great sight fishing and catch two nice reds.

So Many Ways to Mess Up

I love poling into really shallow water, seeing a big fish feeding, casting to it, then watching it eat my fly. When you set the hook, it takes

There is a redfish swimming in the middle of this frame. Its back is a slight hump with a wake trailing after.

off in the only direction available, doing its best to empty all the line off my reel spool. It's an accomplishment because there are so many things to go wrong at each step.

First of all, you have to find a shallow area in which fish are present. Not all flats will have fish nor do all fish use flats. It's a limiting proposition. Usually if you can locate a flat near where fish are caught by gear anglers at other stages of the tide, fish will use it when the tide is right for you. Some flats are best at low tides. These are the ones that are completely covered at higher water but some part of them is exposed at low water. Some flats are best at high tide. Those flats are the ones that only have water on them at high tides during full and new moon periods. Moon tides are when the most water moves and the current flows fastest.

When it's this shallow, fish can't help but disturb the surface when they feed. Here, a redfish nabs a small minnow near an oyster bank.

After you find a good flat, how will you access it? If you have a boat, it needs to be a shallow-draft skiff. A kayak works as long as you can get there in a reasonable amount of time. Often, flats that are close to access areas get a lot of pressure. That makes the fish spooky. If you don't have a boat, finding flats that you can reach by car to wade is a big problem. Another issue is the bottom composition. If it's too soft, you can't wade. This is an issue from a boat as well. You can park your boat and wade, but only if the flat is hard sand. Watch out for stingrays too. The shallow-draft skiff with a poling platform is the best option if you are going to be doing a lot of flats fishing. The best ones float shallow and make minimal sound when being poled. You'll want a graphite push pole as well. There are a lot of them out there; the best are Stiffy Push Poles.

On extreme lunar high tides, the shallow water will be well back in the spartina grass.

Another challenge is the fact that, to catch a fish in the shallows, you need to see the fish first. There is no real substitute for experience. Somebody who's been doing it for years will see fish that a novice will never see. A good guide will locate the fish by telling you to point in the right direction with your rod tip, perhaps referencing a clock with 12:00 at the bow.

Captain David Edens of Flycast Charters in St. Simons Island, Georgia, says, "Lots of times I see a school a long way off and point it out to my clients. I am poling my butt off to get them there, but they are looking all around at the birds, dolphins, oysters, etc. When we get there they miss the shot because they can't find the fish. Don't take your eyes off the water." You still may never see the fish until it bites your fly; it all depends on the depth, clarity, light level, wind, waves and bottom color.

On a windless, bright, sunny day with a white sand bottom in clear water that's less than 8 inches deep, you may see whole fish as they ghost across the flat. They will appear as darker-colored shapes that are moving. Fish don't stop moving. Logs don't stop being still. On windy days with partly sunny skies and murky water over 12 inches deep, the only chance you may have is if a fish tips down to feed and its tail breaks the surface. There are a lot of variables, but the first time you see a big fish in 5 inches of water feed on a crab, you'll never forget it.

Presenting the Fly

Presenting the fly is the last obstacle. It's a big one. Again, there are a lot of things that can go wrong. Ryan Rice of Flyline Media in Charleston, South Carolina, is known for his great videos of redfish eating flies in very shallow water. You can find them on Vimeo. He says, "It's all about the cutoff." You have to be able to ascertain the way the fish is pointed, how fast it's swimming, and how far you need to cast from its face.

Then make an accurate cast and be able to know if the fly was eaten or refused. Hopefully, you'll then hear Ryan say, "Strip...Strip... Strip . . . he ate it! Hit him!"

TAILS GALORE

I met up with my buddy Chris on a summer afternoon in August. That evening's tide was going to be perfect for tailing redfish on the grass flats. The only trouble was the huge storm cloud hanging

Any old port in a storm.

right over us as we got together. It had been raining on and off all day, but we thought we could get a weather window. My boat was out of commission with a trailer issue, so we were using his kayaks. After paddling out, we got to the area where we would spend an hour or so casting around before the tide got high enough to fish the grass flats.

We saw several things happen but not enough to get excited about. It was then we figured that big, black cloud was going to pass right over us, dumping rain in sheets. What to do? Since we didn't have an outboard motor to get us away from the storm, we were stuck. Then I remembered that the creek held a duck blind. Any old port in a storm, right? We dragged ourselves out of the kayaks and into the blind. It just so happened that Chris had a few cold ones in his pack. We enjoyed listening to the rain come down in the relative safety of the blind and enjoyed an ice-cold beer. Thanks, duck hunter dudes!

After the rain passed, the tide was just about perfect. We paddled where we wanted to start and saw a tail almost immediately. I left Chris and paddled around the corner to find a fish right

They can move so softly and slowly that they don't even leave a ripple.

away myself. I promptly hit it in the face, sending it scooting. Chris had no better luck with the one he had seen. Around the next corner we saw another. I let Chris have that one, then found two fish tailing. I wasn't going to mess this one up so I got out of the kayak and began my stalk. When I was about 80 feet out, I started my cast. As I let it go, the fish dropped out of sight. I could no longer see its tail. This happens when the fish takes on a more horizontal position. It's not a problem on a sunny day in a boat but not great on a cloudy day while wading.

The fly dropped and I hoped it was right because I couldn't see the fish. There was a slight swirl and I set the hook instinctively. The fish was on! It made a nice run and pulled hard for a few minutes, then was done. I snapped some quick photos with the smart phone and off he went. It was a memorable evening indeed.

Negative Tides Present Opportunity

A negative low tide occurs when the water is actually lower than the average depth at a normal low. For boaters, this means caution is needed when navigating through unfamiliar waters. For a fly rodder looking for redfish in an area that does not have very clear water (like around my home), it means the flats that are usually under 3 to 4 feet of water may end up being devoid of water or have only a few inches. This tends to concentrate the fish.

I also like to look for "crawlers" on negative lows. I found some on a ridiculously hot day when the temperature flirted with 100°F.

Shrimp flies tend to get eaten in almost any situation by inshore fish.

A school of redfish was working the edge of a shallow channel, busting small minnows along a shoreline. It was actually too shallow for me to get my boat back to where I could see them. Luckily, this was actually in a spot where the bottom is firm enough to wade, although many anglers don't realize this because it's usually deep under water. If they do get out of the water in a spot that is deep enough to float their boat, the mud will suck them down. Even if you are wading, having a shallow-draft poling skiff is the only boat that's skinny enough.

I was mesmerized watching the fish as they pushed into the shallows with their backs and tails out. One time there were about a dozen fish in water so shallow that when they tried to eat my fly they had to turn sideways but could not get the fly in their mouth. Any lightly weighted fly that resembles a small shrimp would work in that situation but I happened to be using a size-2 Seaducer. I usually find it to be a perfect shrimp imitation that gets eaten in almost any shallow-water situation. It was a good day, but afterward, it sure was nice sitting in the A/C sipping an ice cold beverage.

Skiff 101

Let's say you've taken the plunge and bought a fancy new poling skiff. That's great! Now you can get in the shallows after the sneaky redfish you just know are back in there. You figure you'll check it out by yourself the first time out. You get to the spot, the boat floats shallow, and you are pretty sure you just saw a fish tailing way in the back. Perfect! You climb up on the platform with your trusty push pole . . . wait a second . . . where are you going to put your rod?

With no clear choice, you lay it down in front of your feet. Now you start to pole. Hmm . . . the boat seems to be slapping the water a little. That never happened when you went out with the builder for a test

A well-appointed flats skiff.

run. You will worry about it later. For now that fish seems to be moving slowly further away from you, so you lean on the pole a little to catch up. As you get closer the fish seems to move faster, but still is not spooked. Now you are in range. What are you going to do with your push pole? You stick it between your knees and reach down for your rod.

You look up again and you can't see your fish anymore . . . oh there it is, it's moved further away but you can still reach it with a long cast. Now the push pole is sliding between your knees, so you have to get a better hold on that. The fish is a little farther now. You snap out a long cast at the edge of your range. Pretty good but not really where you hoped it would end up. You are just behind the fish and strip line quickly to make one last cast before it gets away for good. Now the push pole is sliding down again. You reach down to adjust it again but you drop it. The rattle it makes against the platform shatters the air. Then you drop your rod, watching helplessly as it clatters into the cockpit. Needless to say, your fish has become a memory as it torpedoes toward the next zip code. What could have been done differently to give this adventure a successful outcome? Let's break it down.

First, a well-designed poling skiff is meant to pole best from the platform with another person on the front casting deck. When a sole angler poles from the tower, the bow lifts and the stern squats. This does two things: it enables water to slap against the underside of the hull and the boat now needs more water to avoid scraping the bottom. Both of these make noise and push fish away.

The solution is to pole from the bow. Many builders are putting smaller forward platforms on the bow. Alternatively, the new

A push pole in hand and clip for it on the belt, a stripping basket with notches cut into it, and the line stripped in, allows you to cast quickly to any fish.

premium-quality coolers are strong enough to stand on after being strapped down. When you see a fish, you can get quite close since your boat will be even shallower than usual. Of course, you can get some wave slappage off the stern so you have to pole downwind. Then it's a matter of making a slight push to the side when you are in casting range so the rest of the boat is not in your way while you are putting down the pole and picking up the rod.

Speaking of which, how are you going to do that exactly? It takes a combination of the right equipment and a little practice. First, put your rod where you can get it easily. There are several products that allow you to wear your rod on your hip using a belt and a clip. I use a stripping basket with notches cut in the top to hold the rod. The push pole can easily be clipped onto a belt-wearable device designed specifically for this purpose. There are a few on the market—I have a Polemate-brand clip. Now when you are poling, you have your rod ready and stowed in a safe fashion. If you see a fish, clip the pole to your belt and grab the rod from its easily accessible location. With just the right push, the boat will pivot slightly as you make the switch. The added benefit of this is that as the boat pivots you will be 16

This beautiful 5-pound speckled trout was cruising a shallow flat.

feet closer to the fish. Now if the fish moves away, your push pole will be right at hand to make a quick adjustment. At this point it depends on your casting skills, which we've already discussed.

Chapter Twenty

Wading the Flats

The schooling redfish in front of me looked like they were packed together in a can. I was wading a small tidal creek with a firm, sandy bottom during a negative low tide. The creek channel only held half the water normally there, so the fish had

Winter wading means waders and warm clothing.

no place to go. The hardest part was making a cast that didn't spook the fish and also didn't hang up on the spartina grass that at this low stage of the tide was actually above my head. Also, did I mention that it was January? Yeah, that's important.

In winter, redfish will gather into big schools, packing together in one spot. Fish that had been spread out in singles, doubles, or smaller schools all year will come together when the temperature drops. When you are looking for them, you will swear there are no fish anywhere, but if you find them it will be like striking gold, at least with the color. If you do it right, you can catch fish all day. Doing it right means putting on some waders and going slow and steady. Staying in the boat at low tide and fishing over a big school will probably get you a couple fish. Then the inevitable will happen and the fish will spook after seeing the boat over and over, or you will mistakenly float over the school, sending them all away.

This happens especially in narrow creeks, like the one I was fishing that day. If the bottom is hard enough, put on your waders and

This expert angler used stealth and expert casting ability to wade up on this memorable high tide redfish.

get after them that way. I was able to figure out the angle of my cast. It took about an 80-foot shot but I dropped my small, white bait-fish pattern in front of one. He nailed it and away he went. It was a lovely 6-pounder and the water around me was teeming with them. I released him to feed and fight again then went after the rest.

Charles Smith's Words of Wisdom

If you ever are poling a boat on a very windy day, you will understand how difficult it can be to maneuver yourself into just the right position. Forget about gently slowing down, and if you don't have a pushpin anchor, forget about stopping. Sometimes you can't even slow down. This is another time when you will have to get out of the boat.

I was lucky enough to meet Charles Smith on a trip to the Bahamas years ago. Yes, that Charles Smith, the one the Crazy Charlie bonefish fly is named after. I bought him a beer or two and let him talk. He said something in particular that has always stayed with me, "When it's windy, you got to get out the boat. The bonefish, he see the boat when it move too fast and the fly don't look right." He was right, as he was about a lot of other things too. When it's super windy, your boat will move so quickly you won't be able to do all the things needed, like control the drift, cast accurately, or present the fly properly. So if it's feasible and you know there are fish around, get out. Get some good flats boots and use a stripping basket. Now you are slowed down enough to do it right.

When I went bonefishing on Oahu, Captain Jesse had us wading almost exclusively. It was really breezy. The flats we were fishing were small because the wind was pounding the bigger outside flats. If we had stayed in the skiff, we would have covered the whole thing in ten minutes. As it was, there were so many fish on this small flat that we would have missed shots at literally dozens of bones. So we waded. We never went more than ten minutes without seeing a fish. I caught four, broke off another, missed a few bites, and even had small trevally steal my fly from under a bonefish's nose several times. It was wading that allowed us to spend the time to do it right.

Go Stealthily

Now this should go without saying, but I'm going to say it anyway. Those fish are in that shallow water to feed, so if you make a good cast, they'll probably eat it. They don't live there, preferring deeper water most of the time. Being shallow makes all fish nervous because they have a deep fear of predators above them, like egrets, osprey, raccoons, pelicans; it's a long list. You have to approach the same way that a heron does. Stealthy, slow, and quiet. I've started wearing muted colors and even a camouflage hat to match my surroundings. I wear a sky blue one when I am going to be fishing big flats on a clear day, and a "camo" colored hat for the marsh. It may not matter that much but it makes me happy.

Watch your step. Years ago I was told to walk with "cotton feet," which makes sense. Fish can feel vibrations, so if you are pushing big waves across a flat, they know that is unnatural. Don't cast your line over the fish. That'll spook them for sure, just as will casting your line so it falls across their backs. This is called "lining the fish." It's pretty much a guaranteed spook-out.

Let me sum up: be slow, be quiet, be accurate. Wading will get you closer to the fish than you can get with a skiff, and you can be extra stealthy. Or you can mess it up and blow every fish off the flat for as far as you can see. But, you know, no pressure or anything!

This young angler was able to stealthily wade up to a school of redfish feeding on the edge of a flat that the wind prevented us from approaching otherwise.

Expertly playing the fish.

Almost there.

Just about.

Success!

There's a big sandy patch in front of a beautiful waterfront mansion just outside of Honolulu. It's near a wildlife preserve and a city park. If you've ever been there you know what I'm talking about. It's a pretty well-known spot to the locals there. This sandy patch draws some big bonefish. It was my first day fishing and I had seen a few big tails but had not gotten a good shot at any. I had stopped to look around and noticed a guy was on the balcony looking out over the water reading his morning paper, drinking coffee. I thought that it was a perfect spot for my dream house for sure.

I looked back at the water to see a huge bonefish swimming right at me. I dropped a 20-foot cast that would have been good back home for redfish but was much too close for bonefish. The roostertail that fish put up when he bugged out of there was amazing.

From behind me I heard, "Guess you got a little too close to that one." Thanks for the advice, Mr. Rich Dude with a Mansion.

Two days later I was in the same spot. Tide was perfect. Almost low tide, plenty of light. This time I saw my fish from quite a distance away. I dropped it perfectly about 10 feet in front of him and gave it a nudge. He swam over just as confident as you please. It's like being connected to a live wire when you hook up. He ran out my whole fly line in seconds. I got him most of the way back in then he did it again. I finally landed him right in front of Mr. Rich Dude's coffee patio for some sweet redemption, but he was long gone. By wading slowly and with a good approach on flats like this, you can move quietly enough and present a fly just right to connect.

Chapter Twenty-One

Fishing for Deep Feeders

The depth-finder screen showed more striped bass beneath my boat than tourists in Times Square on a sunny June Saturday. There were six boats within sight of me. One using fly tackle, two casting jigs and the others bait soaking. You'd think it would be a simple matter to get a bite but you'd be wrong. Nobody was catching fish but me. There was obviously something different that I was doing. I was using an 8-weight fly rod with a sinking line and a big bucktail streamer fly. I was getting a follow, hit, or hookup on every cast while the other anglers looked on in amazement. I could hear one guy say, "Why you think them there bugs on a fly rod are working when we can't get bit on live bait?" Ten seconds later I set the hook into another feisty striper.

Merits of a 350-Grain Line

If you want to catch a fish on a fly in deep water, you have to make sure that the fish sees your fly. Then you have to trigger a strike. When casting to schools of fish that are holding deep, you want to maximize the amount of time the fly is in the zone in front of or just above their faces. This means a sinking line. Integrated sinking

A school of fish shows up solid on the depth-finder screen.

shooting heads are the easiest to use and are readily available. I used to make amazingly effective custom shooting heads out of lead core trolling line. They sank fast, stayed deep, and were less expensive. Trouble arose when there was a problem such as a hang-up or break off while fishing. If you couldn't tie nail knots in the boat, you were out of the game. Even though I was able to re-rig on the spot, it was time consuming. Now I primarily use 350-grain sinking lines from any of the major manufacturers. They are easy to cast and the newer ones offer excellent performance. I've tried the full-sinking lines and I don't enjoy casting them.

Often when we get bonito runs in the spring along the Carolina coast, the fish won't show on the surface; rather they hold over high-relief structure. That means shipwrecks. Drift over the wreck and look for marks over the structure off the bottom. Cast a 350-grain sinking line with a streamer tied on a long-shank 1/0-size hook. Start your cast when the running line is all on the deck at your feet and the shooting head is just to your hand. Pick up and false cast once or twice until the head is just outside the rod tip and you can feel the rod loading. Shoot the whole length of your cast. Don't attempt to false cast very much of the running line outside the rod tip because it will collapse and not cast very well. Also, you might get hit in the back of the head.

A chartreuse-over-white streamer is a good one to start with. Add some flash. Cast it upstream and count it down until you think it's just over the fish by experimenting with your count relative to the listed sink rate of the line (see Chapter 9). Strip it back with a hard pulling motion. When you get a bite, the line will come tight fast. Be prepared to give line when the fish wants to run or you'll get busted off. Let the line slip through your fingers while still maintaining slight tension. Otherwise the loose line will jump up into the stripping guide in a huge knot and you'll get busted off again or worse, break a guide. When all the loose line is off the deck, then you can play the fish from the reel.

MAKE THE FLY JUMP

To trigger a strike you've got to make the fly jump. On a floating line that's easy. You can see the fly and watch its movement. With a sinking line you've got to strip with your line hand as if you were punching someone that is standing right behind you. If you're not punching it, the fly isn't jumping and you probably won't get a bite.

I was in Nantucket fishing for stripers on a steep beach with other fly anglers around. I cast my 350-grain line, started my punch retrieve, and hooked up on the third pull. It felt like someone grabbed the line and was trying to take it. I caught stripers in the 25-inch range on twenty straight casts. I was glad to help the two guys that asked me. One had the right gear and was using it wrong so I showed him. The other did not and I let him use mine. They each proceeded to catch fish.

The same technique is useful for false albacore holding deep. They show on your depth-finder screen as streaks moving up and down. Sometimes you can catch amberjack this way too. Other times they will follow behind your fly but won't commit. This is when you go the other route for catching deep fish—a popper. For big offshore fish, a 1-inch diameter popper with a deeply cupped face will make enough noise to get their attention. Make it loud. These fish are used to it. I've done it for amberjack, striped bass, albies, and of course bluefish. I would bet that casting one of those B.A. Poppers over yellowfin tuna would earn you a reaction as well. Anytime you can see fish less than 30 feet from the surface and you can't get them to hit a streamer on a sinking line, give it a shot.

The amberjacks were right there. Right there! Twenty feet down. They were all over the depth finder. They wouldn't hit a deep fly or even a jig. "Here goes one last shot," I said as I threw a long cast with a big popper. On the third cast, I was getting disheartened when I saw the silver flashes appear, darting up and fighting the other out of the way to get the vulnerable, blurping treat. The water blew up 10 feet away from the boat. "Okay, so that works," I said.

Amberjacks come up from down deep to chase a popper. There are at least four in this picture.

Chapter Twenty-Two

Fishing for Surface Feeders

What are you going to do now?

You've seen the pictures and heard the stories, either in magazines or on the television fishing shows. It's surface-feeding fish—schools of them, acres even, busting on top—a vision that sets the angler's heart hammering in anticipation. Sooner or later you will be confronted with it. Albies. Bluefish. Striped bass. Largemouth bass (yep, they do it too, in big lakes and reservoirs). Spanish mackerel. Jacks of all kinds. If a game fish swims in a school and primarily feeds on small minnows that also school, they will eventually do it where their feeding activity shows on top. Hopefully, you will be there, fly rod in hand, ready to go.

Captain Brendan McCarthy of Urban Flyguides in New York City, fly-fishing guide to the stars, says, "although not always the way to catch the biggest fish, surface feeds are a drug most anglers cannot say no to. They are, after all, what drew most fly and light-tackle anglers to the sport in the first place."

Why They Feed on Top

Those birds know what they are doing and you had better also.

What will make fish feed or "break" on top? Large schools of baitfish trigger these frenzies. When do these large schools come together? Mostly during the heavy migrations in the spring and fall. Does that mean you can't run across some in the middle of summer or even in winter? Of course not; it happens frequently. Honestly, the only hard-and-fast rule that exists in all of fishing is that there are no hard-and-fast rules. What we prefer to do is play percentages and look for the things that generally happen annually in that particular season.

Racer blues travel up the coast in spring. They are hungry and eat everything they see.

So we'll look for fish busting on top in the spring and fall. Springtime fish are famished. It's not uncommon to find schools of bluefish that would ordinarily weigh over 10 pounds but are under 6 or 8 pounds because they are so skinny. The old salts used to call these fish "racers," because they are skinnier than racing dogs. If you happen across a school of blues like this, you will likely catch so many that your arm will hurt and your clothes will be covered in slime. Take a shower as soon as you get home. You will have had fun but you will stink! These fish will hit anything.

In North Carolina we see schools of Atlantic bonito along our coast in the spring. These fish are also very aggressive. In fact if you have ever fished for bonito during fall in New England, you will not believe how easy it is to get a bite from these spring fish.

Fall Is "Primo"

Fall is the "primo" time to find busting fish. I have found schools of September redfish in the marsh busting on bay anchovies. Spanish mackerel slash silversides off Cape Lookout in October. False

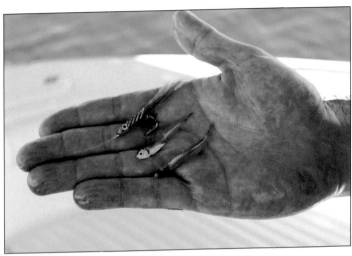

Classic false albacore pattern for fall fishing, when tiny bay anchovies are thick.

albacore feasting on anything they can find in November. They push the bait together, then drive them to the surface where they erupt in a silvery shower trying to evade the hungry predators. Up and down the coast the same thing will be happening with different species of fish at the same time. Wherever schools of gamefish meet schools of baitfish, be there.

You can do this on foot but to really get after them you need a boat, such as a nice center console. Around Cape Lookout you can get away with a smaller boat than you might in other places, because the shape of our east- and west-running beaches shelter us from the prevailing northerlies in the fall. Other places you will probably need something more in the 20-foot or larger range. Scale your tackle to the fish. For bluefish, Spanish mackerel, or albacore under 6 pounds, you can use an 8-weight rod. For false albacore over 10 pounds, I

Sometimes the bait is big and a large, bright fly is necessary.

prefer a 10-weight. See tarpon around a mullet school? Better get a 12-weight.

Finding the Fish

First, be on the lookout for diving birds. The right kind of birds doing the right kind of aerials can put you right on the fish. Most of the time you can forget pelicans; not always, but most of the time. If they are sitting in a group and dipping their beaks in the water, you should check them out because that means a lot of minnows are balled up on top right there.

Gannets are good for finding striped bass when big menhaden are around. The gannets will dive on them from above, while the stripers feed from below. Primarily, look for gulls. If you see the gulls doing what I call a "dance on the water," you have found that which you seek. Get over there. Now. Gamefish will be beneath them driving Atlantic silversides, bay anchovies, or peanut menhaden to the surface.

Fly Fishermen Make Smart Approaches

How you approach the fish at the last moment before the cast can make the difference between a hookup or disappointment. If the water is really calm and you're way offshore, if you get too close you'll spook them. If there is nobody else around, you'll want to see if you can shut down and drift to them. If there are numerous other boats, you may have to be more aggressive, especially if others seem to be rushing the fish.

If the fish are along the shore, you will often be able to figure out which way they're going—left or right. If that's what's indeed happening, and again you are alone, they'll get to you. You may have to bounce up and back a little, but again try not to come in too hot. If the schools are big and feeding hard on top (it makes a really cool noise like rapids in a river), then you can relax and take your time. If the schools are small, you might have to hurry. Sometimes it will seem like they only are on top for as long as it takes to get there. Then they will pop up in the place you just left. The conditions will change every day. Don't have a preconceived notion of what you will have to do. Some days you will be able to be relaxed about it. Some days you will have to put the throttle down and "run and gun." I used to have a 17-foot center console with a 90-horsepower motor on it. If there were a lot of boats around and the fishing devolved into bumper boats, or what I call "NASCAR" fishing, that boat always got me there first. Thrust to weight ratios, right?

Now they're right in front of you. Get your fly into the melee as far as you can. Don't be satisfied with casting to the edge. Get all the way into the middle where you will see the fish. They'll be coming out of the water. Zipping by just under the surface. Minnows will be popping out, gulls dipping in. Nature! Chaos! Zip your fly in there, get the line tight, and start moving it. These fish are seeing minnows flee for their lives so your fly needs to be doing the same thing. If you don't get bitten, which happens when there are so many targets, cast again. Keep casting until you are hooked up or until the fish go down. If for some reason the fish go down and you didn't get a bite, cast again but move the fly slower. Make it look like a straggler left over from the scrum. Many people forget it, but this trick has gotten me a lot of fish over the years.

You got a bite! Now the fish is going to take off. Make sure that your line is clear of the reel, you're not standing on the line and, you are smiling because this is nothing but fun. Yeehaw!

That first run is what it's all about.

Chapter Twenty-Three

Places to Visit

When you go to new places, you get to go after fish you normally don't get to pursue.

Magazines and TV shows are good for showing us great fishing spots. There are coastal fisheries all over the world that are amazing to visit with a fly rod. Southern Louisiana is known for its giant redfish in shallow water. Islamorada in the Florida Keys is famous for giant tarpon in the spring. Guiding in Alaska is a never-ending parade of trout and salmon. Bonefishing is great in the Bahamas and you may want to try Oahu's o'io (bonefish) someday. Cape Cod, Massachusetts. Montauk, New York. But let's focus on some great places to check out between North Carolina and North Florida.

Roanoke River

I had invited the owner of Pete's Tackle Shop in Morehead City to visit me on the Roanoke River for a day of striped bass fishing. Pete Allred had never experienced this fishing so I wanted to show it to him. After a short session of showing him how to handle the sinking fly line, Pete was soon making lovely casts. He was a natural angler who picked up new things quickly; he figured out how to cast and retrieve his fly almost immediately.

Pete ended up catching dozens of stripers in that evening session and we had a great time. It's a great memory of a friend who is no longer with us. Weldon, North Carolina, is the self-proclaimed "Rockfish Capital of the World." The Roanoke River where it flows through town is host to a tremendous spawning migration of striped bass in April and May. While the numbers of returning fish seem to have dropped off the past few years, it is a scene that is worth checking out because in no other place will there be that many fish jammed into that small a space. If you want to catch a striped bass on a fly, this is pretty much a sure thing. When we were done, we hit the world-famous barbecue place in town and I may have cleaned off the buffet myself.

Cape Lookout

The very first fish I caught on a fly in saltwater was a Spanish mackerel at Cape Lookout, North Carolina. For that reason and a whole lot more, it holds a special relevance for me. Chris Batsavage is now the chief flounder guy for the North Carolina Division of Marine Fisheries, but back then he was a grad student at East Carolina University. We went out from Harker's Island and as soon as we could see Barden's Inlet we saw the Spanish busting little glass minnows.

At that time I had never caught one on a fly. All I knew was they liked things to be moving at warp speed. So I cast into the mix and retrieved so fast that I thought I was going to lose an arm. It wasn't fast enough. The little buggers just casually swam under my fly and kind of milled around. I retrieved even faster next time and then I was rewarded. Since then I've always told people that when fishing flies for Spanish macks, retrieve the fly as fast as you think you can, then go a little faster. It wasn't a huge fish, but it got me hooked. Later we had a great grill session with fresh mackerel fillets.

Wrightsville Beach

Bill Douglass is an old buddy and a great guy who lives in Wilmington, North Carolina. He called me up with an invite on a bonito excursion out of Wrightsville Beach. Never say no to invitations like this! After driving down there in the dark, we ran out Masonboro Inlet at first light. The fish were stacked on the reef and at one point we could see feeding fish on the surface spread out over several acres. We cast to busting fish for the first hour or so. When that slowed down we went to sinking lines drifting over the reefs while casting streamer flies. We caught fish until 9:00 o'clock when we headed in for a great cup of coffee at a local roaster with amazing cinnamon rolls.

Charleston

Everybody knows that Charleston, South Carolina, is a great place to visit. You can enjoy the charm of the old downtown and eat amazing food at some famous restaurants. To a fly angler these are just sidelines to why you really visit Charleston: redfish in the huge estuary system. It is a great fishery that surrounds the city extending for miles in every direction. There are probably more flats boats per capita of any area in the Carolinas here. This is a great indicator of the high-quality shallow-water fishing. I recently visited the area with my buddy Pete. I poled my boat back into an area a local friend had recommended.

As soon as we came around the last corner, feeding reds surrounded the boat. They were spread out in a pocket and feeding on shrimp. I could see the shrimp jumping, followed by a splash and a loud *pop*. One overly aggressive fish even ended up on the mud bank and slid back in. Reaching out with a long cast in the shallow water was usually followed by an immediate strike on my shrimp fly. Pete and I caught a couple of nice reds then headed back for some awesome biscuits before heading home.

Jacksonville Beach

I had met Dave Borries while working the winter fishing show circuit. He invited me to spend a few days fishing his home waters near Jacksonville Beach, Florida. We headed out on a low-tide session that we reached after a mazelike run through a variety of small creeks. We got to a spot with an oyster bar reaching into a deeper hole that had the only water over 6 inches left in the whole area. The fish were stacked up on the bar smacking shrimp. Dave gave me a spoon fly that he had tied. It was pretty much a done deal since I had an 8-pound redfish to the boat soon after. I also caught a flounder on a fly that day and even a nice speckled trout to get my inshore slam. Dave was a chef at a local bistro so I was later treated to a great meal. Are you noticing a trend yet?

Several other areas worth checking out are Georgetown, Cape Romain, and Hilton Head in South Carolina; the Golden Isles and Savannah in Georgia; and even a little south of Jacksonville, Florida, to St. Augustine. There are acres upon acres of spartina marsh. You'll find spots full of fish, pristine beaches with endless possibilities, and inlet after inlet. Don't let me limit your explorations. Get out and find your own.

Chapter Twenty-Four

Tides, Wind, and Weather

Putting all the pieces together makes for happy anglers.

You just had the greatest day ever! There was a huge school of fish in a gorgeous cove that ate your fly so much they chewed all the fuzz off. You caught so many your buddies will have to get the smile off your face with a crowbar. Facebook and Instagram are now packed full of pictures of you and a fish, a fish and your rod, a fish on your lap, and fish with your flies in their mouths. I believe the word the kids are using now is "epic." You are so excited you get your buddy and go to the same place at the same time the very next weekend. The water looks completely different. It's murky, it's a different depth, and the wind is blowing things all around. What's going on?

You have fallen victim to the ever-changing mood of saltwater. When you learn to fish in freshwater, you learn which flies to use, how to read water, and tons of other things. One thing you don't have to contend with on a trout stream or a bass lake is tide. Tide rules all. Here's what you need to know.

Study Your Tides

That perfect day you had? You hit it just right and lucked into it. Get out your smartphone. Tap the "AyeTides" app I told you to download; you did download it, right? Figure out what the tide condition was on that perfect day then find a date in the future that's similar. That will get you started. Do some research. Ask guys you meet at fly and tackle shops what they consider to be a good tide for the type of fish you want to catch. It's not just in shallow-water situations, fish in the ocean will often use certain areas and either bite or not bite due to tidal conditions. If fishing around a wreck, fish will move to the side of the wreck that appeals to them because of the current direction. The absolute best time to fish an inlet is during the outgoing tide and the faster it's moving, the better.

LEARN THE EFFECTS OF WIND

Now download a marine weather app. Look for days with wind conditions that match your casting ability and where you are fishing. Be aware that sometimes tide will be affected by wind. Strong wind will often blow water into or out of an area. This means that even though the forecast tide is one thing according to the chart, it may be quite different with the wind. If the wind is blowing toward your fishing area, it may be deeper and if it is blowing from your area it may be shallower. Wind can also turn clear water murky. When the wind shifts around and starts blowing 15 knots into your favorite creek, you're probably not going to even see the bottom. Also be aware of light conditions. Sunny skies will make it easier to spot fish in sight-fishing situations. When the sun comes out on a day where the clouds are your nemesis, it will seem like you had been in a dark room and somebody turned on the lights.

Basically, every two weeks you can expect the tides to be similar, with the time moving back an hour or so each time, until eventually it changes to the opposite of what it was the first time. Yeah, I know

These ibises know the tides and the weather without having to be taught.

that's confusing. Check a tide chart. The final thing you need to consider is the moon phase. The tidal currents will run fastest during the week surrounding the full-moon period, pretty hard during the new moon, and then slowest during the weeks between those. Why the heck does that matter? When there is more current, the little critters that gamefish like to pursue get pushed around by the water more; they become easier targets. The big fish know this and they feed more because when it's easier to eat, we all eat more. It's like being at a Chinese buffet. You don't normally eat a plate of sushi followed by a plate of teriyaki chicken and then some pot stickers, but there it is just sitting there. So it is with fish.

FISH ENJOY A BUFFET

"I am Ms. Big Fish and I don't always get to hang out in a favorite spot snapping up glass minnows with ease as they get swept down the current. But here they are so I'm going to get one. Got it. Another. Yum. Oh there's another one that looks even easier to grab than all the rest. I am the biggest fish in this school so I am going to get it before all the other little goofballs do. They can't swim as fast as I can in today's heavier currents. Chomp. Oh hey, why is

Knowledge of tide and wind paid off for a great day of speck fishing.

this one pulling on me? I've got to get out of here. Shake my head to

Letting one go for next time.

get this thing off me. Hey, what is reaching down to grab me. Now I can't breathe. What the heck are those giants doing? Gasp. Gasp. Oh phew, the giant thing is putting me back where I can breathe again. Out of here! Free at last."

At least that's how I imagine their minds operate. Probably not, but you get the general picture. Greater current during the full- and new-moon phases create more opportunity for large fish to feed and therefore more chances for you to catch a really big one.

Conclusion

I hope you have gotten something out of reading this book. I tried really hard to include enough information to get you going. I didn't give it all away, but hopefully you'll be able to go catch some fish that you couldn't previously. Let me add that if you are fishing on the coast you need to be involved in some sort of conservation effort or other resource group. Even if it's just sending $25 to your favorite conservation group, do something constructive. The en-

Is this the future we want for our fisheries?

vironment and fish are under attack on a daily basis from those who would just as soon get a dollar from the water without caring what happens afterward.

One of the biggest problems in saltwater fishing around the globe is unsustainable fishing methods. This includes things like long lines that catch untargeted species, huge seines that catch untargeted species, factory trawlers that catch untargeted species, and last but not least, both drift and stationary gill nets that catch, you guessed it, untargeted species.

Gill Nets and Huge Trawlers

There are two major issues we have been dealing with in my home water of North Carolina: large, deep water trawlers working the shallow depths of Pamlico Sound, and unattended gill nets in shallow water statewide. These industrial-size trawlers are largely responsible for almost wiping out our populations of spot, croaker, and gray trout (weakfish). This is pretty much why I did not include weakfish in this book. There haven't been enough around to be a target species in quite a while outside of a few isolated pockets that I choose to leave alone. Trawling has affected the weakfish, spot, and croaker populations all along the coast. They basically catch 4½ pounds of unwanted and undersized finfish for every pound of shrimp they catch. This kills millions of juvenile fish every year.

The shallow-water gill-net fishery has nearly ended the inshore southern flounder fishery in North Carolina and is wreaking havoc on our red drum (redfish) population as well. It's a fight that is ongoing. If you live in North Carolina and are not yet involved in this fight, please take a few minutes now to do some online research. There is so much more out there than I could even begin to list here. Start by checking out the documentary "Net Effect" that was made in 2015 by WRAL-TV in Raleigh, North Carolina. It is very informative and presents a true, even-handed account of what is really happening to our coastal fisheries. They simply let all the involved parties speak their minds. The commercial interests involved in the gill-net and trawl fisheries did a pretty good job of putting their feet securely in their mouths. They of course tried to backtrack, claiming they were set up or misrepresented, but the camera just lingered on them as they answered the questions asked. This is a fight that is far from over, and the long-term ramifications are huge for fish populations both now and even more in the future.

A True Irony

There is true irony here as well. Florida has long been a leader in progressive fishing regulations. It was the first state to outlaw entanglement netting because regulators realized the value of live fish in the water far outweighs dead fish in a cooler. Recreational fishing with its billion of dollars spent on everything from boats and hotel rooms to tackle and restaurants impacts local economies far greater than does netting and trawling. However, Florida has a water-quality problem that we do not have here in the Carolinas.

The water from Lake Okeechobee used to get filtered by flowing through the Everglades, but to enable more development, it is diverted through canals flowing directly into estuaries on the east and west coasts of the state. This pollution has been ongoing for years with no end in sight. It has the possibility of ruining the great fisheries of Tampa Bay and the Indian River Lagoon.

Or is this the future we want for our fisheries?

So you see there are myriad issues affecting our coastal ecosystems. Now, more than ever before, all things are connected.

A decision that appears plausible may adversely impact something else, whether it is readily apparent at first or not.

Remember, "When the last tree is cut, the last fish is caught, and the last river is polluted, when to breathe the air is sickening, you will realize, too late, that wealth is not in bank accounts and that you can't eat money."

Appendices

Appendix I: Guides I Recommend (North to South)

Capt. Brendan McCarthy: Long Island/New York City, NY
Featured on the *Guide House* TV show. Fishes New York Bight out of Brooklyn. All over Long Island. Striped bass sight-fishing pioneer. Montauk fall blitz.
urbanflyguides.com

Capt. Tom Roller: Beaufort, NC
Inshore and offshore. Redfish on flats. Developed unique amberjack on fly tactics. Cape Lookout false albacore.
waterdogguideservice.com

Capt. David Edens: St. Simons Island, GA
Redfish in skinny. Low-tide schools. High-tide tailers.
flycastcharters.com

Capt. Bryan Pahmeier: Titusville, FL
Sight fishing for very large trout and redfish on a fly. Reds in super clear water of Indian River and Mosquito Lagoon systems.
orlandoflyfishing.com

Capt. Martin Carranza: Miami/Keys, FL

Bonefish in Biscayne Bay. Tarpon in Keys. Sea run Browns in Argentina.

captmartinc.com

Capt. Greg Dini: Florida Keys, FL

Tarpon and Louisiana marsh redfish.

Monster redfish in the Louisiana Marsh. Huge migratory tarpon in Florida Keys in spring.

louisianaflyfishing.com

Capt. Jesse Cheape: Oahu, HI

Bonefishing on Oahu. Best bonefish action in the world that is accessible from a major airport.

hitideflyfishing.com

Appendix II: Some Products I Like to Use

- Copperhead Skiff by Ankona Boats: **ankonaboats.com**
- Flymen Fishing for fishing and tying products: **flymenfishingcompany.com**
- Polemate pole clip: **floridabackcountry.com**
- Stiffy Push Poles: **stiffypushpoles.com**
- Sea Dek non-skid coating: **seadek.com**

Appendix III:
Some Helpful Fly-Fishing Books

This is not a list of references, nor is it meant to be definitive. These are just some books I have on my shelves that have helped me.

Bluewater Fly Fishing by Trey Combs. Species by species breakdown of offshore fly fishing.

Fly Fisherman's Guide to Saltwater Prey by Dr. Aaron Adams. Great breakdown of prey species.

Fly Fishing the Tidewaters by Tom Earnhardt. The first book dedicated to fishing our waters, published twenty years ago.

Fly Patterns by Fishing Guides by Tony Lolli. More fly ideas.

Fly Rodding the Coast and *Fly Rodding Estuaries* by Ed Mitchell. Reading the water like a stream.

Prospecting for Trout by Tom Rosenbauer. How I learned about fly presentation.

Salmon Flies by Paul Jorgensen. Become a better constructor of flies.

Saltwater Flies of the Southeast and Gulf Coast by Angelo Peluso. Lots of fly ideas.

Saltwater Fly Fishing by Lefty Kreh. Covers everything.

The Striped Bass Chronicles by George Reiger. Gamefish management and what's wrong.

Striper Moon by Kenney Abrames. Innovative ideas about tying and presentation.

Universal Fly Tying Guide by Dick Stewart. First fly tying book I ever owned.

Appendix IV: Fly Leader Construction

There are many leader construction formulas out there. This is what works for me. However long your leader is, the heavy butt section should be around 40 percent of the total length. All constructed with monofilament line. The two-digit pounds numbers refer to the break strength of the line.

12-foot inshore for sight fishing redfish, bonefish, speckled trout, etc.
5 feet 30 pound—4 feet 20 pound—3 feet 10 pound (or 12 or 15 depending on fish size)

9-foot inshore for Spanish mackerel, bluefish, or toothy things
4 feet 30 pound—3 feet 20 pound—2 feet 10 pound—1 foot 30 pound fluoro

9-foot heavier for false albacore or mahi
4 feet 40 pound—3 feet 30 pound—2 feet 20 pound

9-foot heavy for cobia or amberjack
4 feet 40 pound—3 feet 30 pound—2 feet 20 pound—2 feet 60 pound fluoro (Note: resist the urge to simply use 60-pound mono as your whole leader. The leader needs to have a point that is of a lighter break strength than your backing or fly line itself so it will break before the fly line or backing.)

Appendix V: Knots

- Reel arbor to backing: Arbor Knot
- Backing to fly line: Albright Special

- Fly line to leader butt: Albright Special or Nail Knot
- Leader construction: Surgeon's Knot
- Tippet to fly: No-Name Loop Knot

Appendix VI: Smartphone Apps for the Fisherman

- AyeTides: Extremely accurate tide algorithm.
- Marine Weather: Great up-to-the-minute weather predictions.
- Hi-Def Radar: Shows exactly where that storm is and where it's going.
- Navionics: Detailed marine charts.
- iHurricane: If a hurricane is coming, this is your friend.
- Instagram: Instant photo sharing.

Appendix VII: Coastal Fishing Towns in the Region

From north to south: Shorelines with southerly ocean currents, sand beaches, and spartina grass marshes that exist from Cape Lookout, North Carolina, to St. Augustine, Florida.

NORTH CAROLINA

Beaufort, Morehead City, Topsail Beach, Wilmington, Wrightsville Beach, Carolina Beach, Southport, Ocean Isle Beach, Holden Beach

SOUTH CAROLINA

Georgetown, McClellanville, Isle of Palms, Mount Pleasant, Charleston, Folly Beach, Edisto, Beaufort, Hilton Head

GEORGIA

Savannah, Tybee Island, Brunswick, St. Simons Island, Jekyll Island

NORTH FLORIDA

Atlantic Beach, Jacksonville Beach, St. Augustine